CW01654822

CONTENTS

Assessment in a Multicultural Society

RELIGIOUS STUDIES AT 16+

a discussion document

Angela Wood

LONGMAN FOR SCHOOLS COUNCIL

1984

Published by Longman for Schools Council
Longman Resources Unit
33-35 Tanner Row
York YO1 1JP

FOREWORD

In this introductory note to this series of documents I would like to make it clear that these are discussion documents which the Schools Council thinks it helpful to publish, and that they are not statements of Schools Council policy. The views expressed in them are those of their authors, and not necessarily the views of the Schools Council.

It is part of the business of the Schools Council to stimulate discussion and ideas within the field of curriculum and assessment; where there is no discussion and no disagreement there is no life. Some of the ideas and views expressed in these documents may be regarded as critical or controversial, but it is the Council's view that discussion of the curriculum and assessment is helpful and leads either to improvements or to a better understanding of what exists in relation to needs and to possible alternatives.

These documents are therefore published in the belief that they may stimulate such discussion, which may or may not lead to changes in assessment, but should lead to a better understanding of the problems involved.

The Schools Council would like to express its thanks to the many people and bodies who have given help with the preparation of this series, and, in particular, to the examining boards for their generous cooperation which included their officers' discussions with the authors, as well as the provision of, and permission to quote from, syllabuses, papers, and examiners' reports.

ARNOLD JENNINGS

Chairman, Examinations Committee
Acting Chairman, Schools Council

INTRODUCTION

Assessment in a Multicultural Society is one of several major projects in the Schools Council's fifth programme of work, Improving the Examinations System. On 25 September 1981 a Schools Council conference on examining in a multicultural society brought together representatives of the GCE and CSE examining boards, teachers, members of Her Majesty's Inspectorate and others actively involved in multicultural curriculum and examination development to discuss the relationship between examining and the needs of a multicultural society. Following the conference, a number of subject specialists were commissioned to write detailed reviews of 16+ examination provision in their subject areas, with particular reference to the needs of a multicultural society. An important consideration governing the timing of the commissions was the concurrent preparation of general and subject specific national criteria for syllabuses, forms of assessment and grading for the proposed single system of examining at 16+. Though, at the time of writing, a final decision on the single system has yet to be made, it seems clear that the national criteria, whether applied to a dual or single system, will play a crucial part in determining the future form that 16+ examining takes.

Both the conference and the ensuing project are part of a much wider series of activities that the Council has undertaken to encourage developments in multicultural education. The Council, for example, has endeavoured to ensure that the 16+ national criteria take into account the multicultural dimension. Other current work concerning the multicultural education of all pupils includes the writing of pamphlets for teachers on resources and on school and classroom practice, the development of materials to enhance sensitivity to cultural diversity and an exploration of models of in-service training of teachers. These activities complement the Council's continued work on the particular needs of children from minority groups, which includes a major project on supporting community languages in primary schools and work on the language development of pupils whose main language or dialect is not standard English.*

Cultural differences which have a religious, linguistic or ethnic basis are potentially a source of considerable conflict, and therefore a matter for serious social, political and educational concern. The Council's programme of work in multicultural education aims to reduce prejudice and hostility towards minority groups, and also to help teachers provide a positive and non-racist learning environment for all their pupils.

---

* This term is used in the sense defined by V. Edwards in her book *Language Variation in the Multicultural Classroom:* 'standard English [is] merely another dialect with high social acceptance and status.'

The Council believes that the development of a multicultural curriculum which includes examples drawn from a wide range of cultures and which avoids presenting a solely Anglocentric view of the rest of the world, can add new opportunities and dimensions to all children's learning. The report in 1981 of an earlier Schools Council project, *Education for a Multiracial Society*, stressed the need to permeate all school subjects with a multicultural perspective, and suggested the following five curriculum guidelines which have been reaffirmed in later Council publications:

1 The curriculum needs to be both international in its choice of content and global in its perspective.

2 Contemporary British society contains a variety of cultural groups. This variety should be made evident in the visuals, stories and information offered to children.

3 Pupils should have access to accurate information about differences and similarities between cultural groups.

4 People from British minority groups and from other cultures overseas should be presented as individuals with every variety of of human quality and attribute. Stereotypes of minority groups in Britain and of cultures overseas, whether expressed in terms of human characteristics, life styles, social roles or occupational status, are unacceptable and likely to be damaging.

5 Other cultures and nations have their own values; whenever possible they should be allowed to speak for themselves so that they can be better understood, and not judged in terms of British or European norms.

It is important that syllabuses and examinations should harmonize with this developing multicultural curriculum. In its evidence to the Government's Committee of Inquiry into the Education of Children from Ethnic Minority Groups, the Council outlined its position with regard to examining within a multicultural society as follows:

> Public examination results are crucial to a majority of pupils. They qualify pupils for admission to higher and further education; they can determine whether or not a candidate will be considered for a particular job. It is therefore essential that all pupils have equal opportunities for demonstrating their qualities and abilities through the public examination system.
>
> The interaction between the curriculum, both 'open' and 'hidden', and examinations is very complex. Curriculum development for the fourth and fifth years of secondary education appears to be slower than for preceding years; in Schools Council Pamphlet 18, *Multi-ethnic Education: the Way Forward*, Alan Little and Richard Willey write that 'A number of authorities and 40 per cent of Headteachers, 50 per cent of those in schools with a concentration of minority ethnic group pupils, reported that examinations restrict curriculum development to reflect a multi-ethnic society.' However, the current preparation for a single system of examining at 16+, based for the first time on nationally agreed syllabus and assessment criteria, presents a crucial opportunity to innovate.

The Council's submission goes on to consider examination provision in a world that is increasingly interdependent and part of a society that is already culturally diverse. It recommends that examinations should be culturally fairer, more culturally diverse and include more and modified examinations with particular cultural emphases. It continues with detailed recommendations as follows:

Towards culturally fairer examinations

In so far as our society, like all societies, reflects in its examination system the dominant cultural values, this operates in all facets of our examination system, be it examination personnel, the syllabuses, the forms of assessment, or the awarding criteria.

The changing nature of British society requires the formulation of criteria relating to:

1 Syllabuses based on a culturally broad selection of knowledge, skills and attitudes.

2 Forms of assessment (for example, projects, course work) which enable teachers to encourage children to follow areas of study which are of particular interest to the children.

3 Content choices of examination questions that are sufficiently varied to enable all candidates to demonstrate their capabilities.

4 The language, particularly the technical and idiomatic, used for examination questions so as to minimize difficulties of comprehension.

5 Stimulus material that is used as part of examination papers and that illustrates a variety of perspectives.

Examiners should be sensitive to the difficulties of candidates in demonstrating abilities when English is not their first language, and marking should be sympathetic to candidates, rewarding attainment demonstrated through various cultural attitudes and responsive to the full range of acceptable language.

Towards culturally diverse examinations

Examinations, and thus the work leading to them, should be more culturally diverse, not only to be culturally fairer to ethnic minorities but also to enrich the lives of all candidates irrespective of their cultural background. Further, in so far as culturally diverse examination courses can influence pupils' attitudes, they can also play a positive, albeit minor role, in furthering international understanding and improving relationships between the various ethnic groups within Britain.

An apparent dilemma facing the examination world, if it wishes to encourage culturally diverse examinations, is the question of syllabus and examination question options. On the one hand, the existence of options allows teachers and candidates to concentrate on their predilections; on the other hand, fewer options ensures that, for example, Geography candidates could not restrict their studies to Europe, as sometimes happens, but also undertake some study of the Third World. Culturally diverse examinations should encourage breadth with opportunities for specialization in depth.

Towards examinations with particular cultural emphases

At present there are some GCE and CSE board-based examinations designed with particular cultural emphases, but current problems are:

1 They are available from only a few boards which the subject teacher may not be able to choose, as the school as a whole does not enter candidates for them.

2 There are more GCE Mode I than CSE Mode I examinations of this type, so the majority of candidates, for whom CSE is designed, are not so well served as the minority.

3 They tend to concentrate on language and literature, and neglect other cultural dimensions, for example: art, music, geography, history.

4 They are readily accessible to candidates from only a small range of cultural backgrounds.

5 They were often designed for a different clientele (for example, candidates from overseas), and have not changed sufficiently to meet new needs.

In order to improve the position, a number of school-based examinations have been developed in recent years, but they tend mainly to be CSE and to have been prepared by schools with a high proportion of ethnic minority pupils to suit the needs of those particular pupils. Thus GCE candidates or pupils in other schools are ill served. In addition, in so far as they are Mode IIIs, they are often dependent upon the continued presence of specific teachers, can be expensive and therefore subject to increasing economic pressure, and are sometimes regarded warily by potential employers.

The examining boards in adapting their procedures to facilitate changes in their examinations are urged to consider whether:

the composition of those examining reflects and meets the needs of a multicultural society

there is any mechanism for regular monitoring of syllabuses and examination papers in the light of multicultural considerations

there is any provision for consultation and for sharing resources with other bodies who have been developing multicultural perspectives.

In considering the role of examining boards in effecting change, the Council's evidence to the Swann Committee of Inquiry continues:

If our examinations are to be modified to meet the changing needs of a multicultural society then a necessary, though not sufficient, requirement is the creation of a consensus recognizing these needs.

Those wishing changes must recognize the genuine difficulties faced by examination boards. Nearly all change requires additional finance and the boards are subject to the economic constraints faced by the rest of the educational world. In addition, some of the examinations might, particularly initially, attract only small candidatures and thus not benefit from economies of scale.

The role of the boards in innovation depends to a large extent on the wishes of their constituent members, who often do not express any desire for change. New ideas and courses are often difficult to evaluate and to relate to existing standards. Examiners and moderators in specialist subjects are not easily available.

However, it should be pointed out that there is much existing good practice to build upon. Several of the examination boards, through their overseas examining, have extensive experience of providing examinations for candidates with differing cultural backgrounds. Also most of the examining boards have specific examples of subject examinations that meet some of the needs of today's multicultural society, and the Welsh Board offers its examinations through the medium of either English or Welsh. Apart from the very wide range of ethnic minority language and literature examinations available, there exist examination subjects such as Indian Music and Dance, and Caribbean, African or Asian Studies.

There are also numerous examples of change within the more traditional subject areas. In Art and Design there are examinations utilizing practical work derived from different cultures and customs; in Biology there are examinations with examples and applications from more than one country; in English Literature examinations offering a selection of American, African and Caribbean texts; in Geography and Environmental Studies, examinations reflecting the changing nature of our society; in History, examinations that give prominence to non-European History and that link local, national and world history to the reactions and concerns of the peoples of the former British Empire; in Home Economics, examinations that recognize the variety of lifestyles of the pupils, and in Religious Education, examinations that include not only the study of Christianity as perceived and practised by a variety of ethnic groups but also the study of other religious faiths.

With careful nourishment these examples can be the seeds of future change.

The commissioning of these subject reports was seen as a small part of the nourishment process. The 'commissionees', all subject experts with experience of multicultural and 16+ examination matters are all, bar one, practising school teachers. They were asked to undertake a six month, part-time, review of existing 16+ examination provision within their subject and to ascertain how far this provision met or could be developed to meet the needs of a multicultural society.

This pamphlet is therefore one of a series which attempts to explore the subject-specific implications of assessment in a multicultural society. Seven of the reports cover the major subjects of Art and Design; Biology; English; History; Home Economics; Religious Studies, and Social Sciences. These seven reports are intended to encourage the development of 16+ examinations within the more traditional subject areas that will draw from a wider range of cultures than hitherto and that are as a result less culturally biased and more empathetic to the multicultural nature of our society. An eighth report covers Urdu, Hindi, and Modern Greek and is intended to encourage the development of 16+ examinations with particular cultural emphases that will both better serve the current and future needs of ethnic minority candidates and also be more accessible to all pupils, irrespective of their cultural backgrounds.

All eight reports are seen, as stated in the Foreword, as discussion documents contributing to a continuing debate. Examining in a multicultural society is a complex and, at times, an emotive undertaking, and we are well aware that the views presented will not exactly mirror those of the reader, indeed we are conscious that some of the opinions expressed by the various authors do not even represent the views of our own committees. But this is to be expected, and is a healthy situation, for there are no easy solutions. It is hoped, however, that the ideas, criticisms, examples of 'good practice', suggestions, etc., presented within the series might help stimulate the debate and serve as catalysts for future examination development.

The first audience for the Assessment in a Multicultural Society series is thus the policy committees and subject panels of GCE and CSE examining boards and all those involved in the formulation of national criteria at 16+, for clearly this audience will play a decisive role in the development of 16+ examinations. It is hoped that the numerous subject-specific propositions within the reports, together with the more general points raised in this Introduction, may help this target group in their development work.

The examining boards, as a result of national criteria and the resulting examination provision, will clearly exert an important influence on the educational provision of all pupils within our schools. However, their potential role, though significant, will be limited; they can, and in many instances do, initiate change but, unless other sections of the educational profession, in particular practising teachers, recognize and indicate the necessity for change, the examination 'industry' is unlikely to move too far forward for fear of distancing itself from its 'customers'.

Thus a second, and in the long term a more crucial audience for the reports must be those teachers and teacher educators who are concerned to relate educational practices to the realities of today's and tomorrow's multicultural society.

This report was written by Angela Wood, a Religious Studies teacher from a large London comprehensive school; there were a number of external constraints (e.g., time, length, focus) placed upon Ms Wood, and a number of limitations decided and imposed by the author herself. Many readers may feel that the work should have been broader in scope or more wide-ranging in outlook; but no apologies are offered for its concentration on the key questions posed by assessment for a multicultural society.

This pamphlet therefore addresses itself to Religious Studies as an optional examination subject at CSE or GCE O-level at present, and in a possible single system 16+ in the future. Clearly, the teaching and learning leading up to such an examination have implications for earlier teaching and learning in the secondary school - and, indeed, at primary and tertiary levels - but these are not the central concern of this pamphlet, however important they may be in themselves.

GEOFF BARDELL
Project Lead Officer

ALMA CRAFT
Coordinator for
Multicultural Education

October 1983

I THE RESPONSE OF RELIGIOUS STUDIES TO MULTICULTURALISM

> Education and religion ... typically enslave and mystify human beings, and prevent them from seeing clearly the structures of injustice of which they are either beneficiaries or victims; but they can liberate human beings. (Richardson, 1977, p.73)

> Whatever is done in the name of religious education should be in some fundamental sense both religious and educative. (Tibble, 1966, p.1)

Any appraisal of Religious Studies in terms of its response to or formation by the multicultural nature of our society inevitably extends beyond itself. It is a subject which has not only become multicultural in character and content, but which also serves to underline the curriculum issues involved in 16+ examining: the nature of knowledge and values, and the relationship between them; the 'culture' of our classrooms; and the educational processes which promote full freedom.

The wider context of Religious Studies is evident on a number of levels. Firstly, the content of Religious Studies in England and Wales has altered dramatically over the last decade or so and there has been a marked (although by no means uniform or complete) shift from Christianity/Bible-based syllabuses to a more phenomenological approach, a descriptive study of the manifestations of world religions. This new direction can be detected in revised GCE O-level and CSE syllabuses of many examining boards. Secondly, this phenomenology has necessarily prompted an awareness of religious pluralism - an appreciation, beyond the factual level, of the world's many religions and the implications this has for religious identity and affiliation, interfaith dialogue and speculation about truth claims within religious traditions. Thirdly, the social problems, personal relationships and moral matters with which Religious Studies, rightly or wrongly, has become concerned are those of a multicultural society; contemporary issues such as Drugs and Nuclear War are being either supplemented or supplanted by Immigration, SUS, and so on. Fourthly, there has been a move in the direction of more 'progressive' or 'open' pedagogies and child-centred approaches, especially at CSE level and particularly as evidenced by the means of assessment for Mode III. These educational styles are increasingly seen as being not only justifiable in their own right but also relevant to the task of developing the person, helping the child to find a faith to live by ('Durham', 1970), creating a sense of the purpose of life. However, Religious Studies, whether of the more traditional kind or more modern, addresses itself to questions of ultimate significance: Why is the world as it is? Can I know what is true? How should we live? What is humanity? These are indeed the proper concerns of education in general and multicultural education in particular.

However, the awareness of multicultural issues has not been welcomed by the Religious Studies world with total approval: there is an element of committed, conservative Christians who feel threatened by the new developments and equally, there are those who would use Religious Studies, as they would the whole multicultural curriculum, as an instrument of social engineering. Neither those opposed to the 'multiness' of religious education nor those committed to political revolution have sound educational reasons for their cause, and what often masquerades as concern for the curriculum is in reality an attempt to promote partisan interests.

> ...[such people] seem to use religious education to fortify political convictions and to score ideological points ... these issues do not belong to religious education ... This may be a negative point, but it is often instructive, and sometimes downright useful, if undressed emperors are told that they are naked. (Gryn, 1978, p.15)

Religious Studies is not only concerned with multiculturalism: it encompasses the nature and form of numinous experiences, such as the essence of religion, worship in the school, spiritual growth, knowledge of the Christian tradition, and contemporary religion. But the purpose here is simply to explore those aspects of the multicultural curriculum which apply to Religious Studies at 16+.

1 Teaching religion and teaching about religion

> The religious educator, standing in one of the most crowded junctions of contending ideas and issues ... both carries forward makind's most ancient traditions and also attempts to elicit a full range of experience. (Martin, 1977, pp.58,59)

> [Religion is] more central than most subjects to what education is all about. (Hull, 1976, p.130)

The single most decisive influence on contemporary British Religious Studies has been the writings of Ninian Smart (especially *Secular Education and the Logic of Religion*) and the related work at the University of Lancaster, where the project Journeys into Religion (Schools Council, 1977) was based from 1969 to 1973. The project outlined three standard approaches to Religious Studies: the confessional or dogmatic, which aims to indoctrinate; the antidogmatic which sees Religious Studies as academic, logical and dispassionate, and would eliminate all subjective elements by emphasizing rational thought and criticism; and the phenomenological or undogmatic approach which seeks to 'transcend the merely informative' so as to 'enter into an empathic experience of the faith of individuals and groups' (Schools Council, 1971, p.21). The latter is supported as the educationally healthiest approach but it requires skill and sensitivity and it is important to be aware of a paradox at the heart of it:

> There is a deep tension between education on the one hand and the religious and secular ideologies on the other. Education is critical, sceptical and enquiring. Religion is passionate, committed and adoring. (Hull, 1974, p.170)

The role of Religious Studies is to embrace both education and religion: to question as well as to accept. Currently, three styles of Religious Studies can be detected in the classroom:

the *neo-confessional* is an attempt to make confessionalism more modern in method and more acceptable in a multicultural society. It tends to be an open-ended form of Christian education which may include some token acknowledgement of other world faiths;

implicit religion abandons the confessional standpoint altogether, and advocates an unrestricted quest for ultimate meaning in life through reflection on actual human experience. This style is most apparent in the thematic study of religion in primary schools or in general Religious Studies at secondary school or in the social sections of Religious Studies 16+ syllabuses;

explicit religion deals with overt phenomena of religious traditions and some alternatives to religious belief, and tries to come to terms with the pluralistic nature of our society in both intellectual and emotional terms.

> The 'implicit' and 'explicit' belong together - the search for meaning and the study of religions. (Schools Council, 1977, p.13)

New religious education is concerned with initiating young people not into *one* religion but into the meaning of religion and religions. Accordingly, any religious tradition should be seen from the point of view of those who belong to it, and descriptions of religious phenomena should not be distorted by externally imposed value judgements: questions of truth and value should be recognized as such.

> There should be no gossip, no stories about a religion which would not be told in the presence of its adherents.
> (Cole, 1978c, p.23)

This is echoed in Wood's belief (1979) that:

> you want to present Jews, Muslims, Hindus in a positive and, if critical,constructively, appreciatively, critical way. At the very least, not say about them things that are not true. (p.28)

The new Religious Studies aims to elicit the social and experiential context of religion and the religious dimension from the experience and reflective powers of the pupil. While the prevailing tradition of the society might warrant dominance in the Religious Studies curriculum, non-religion and irreligion will be present in it, for the strong agnostic and atheistic secular stand in the modern world must clearly be acknowledged.

> The philosophical base must be religion, or religions, not Christianity - or for that matter Islam or Judaism ... the aims must have to do with the understanding of religion rather than conversion to any particular faith or even to a religious view of life. (Cole, 1972, p.23)

In recent years there has been some attempt, especially by Humanists, to replace the term Religious Studies/Education with Education in Stances for Living, which they feel to be a more inclusive term while preserving all the depth, richness, and subtlety of religion. Stopes-Roe (1976) differentiates thus:

> Life-stance: whatever the individual finds to be involved in his response to ultimacy. Religion: a life-stance which finds ultimacy in God - or more generally, finds ultimacy to involve reference beyond the natural world, to the absolute, or to a transcendent order or process. (p.25)

The first curricular manifestation of 'life-stance' was in the Agreed Syllabus* published in the controversial City of Birmingham's Handbook *Living Together* which advocated intellectual development through a 'problem-centred' curriculum, the individual's search for meaning and a concern for the social context of religion. In adolescence,

> Development is attended by the ability to form some kind of 'world view' ... Religious education is concerned with man's attempt to interpret his existence as it is expressed in the adoption of patterns of belief and behaviour. The lessons must therefore be related to life as young people see and know it, must stimulate them to think about their own pattern of living [and] make a real contribution towards their establishing themselves in the adult world. (City of Birmingham Education Committee, 1975, p.C2)

The Birmingham Handbook is not without its critics, however: Taylor (1976) describes it as 'initiation into agnosticism ... an invitation to non-commitment' (p.129), while Cox (1976) accuses it of ignoring

> what may be the major religion of Britain ... a kind of theistic agnosticism ... 'folk religion' [or] 'subterranean theology' ... Does it regard the subject as enabling pupils to shop around among those religious and life stances that appeal to them in order to 'find a faith to live by'? (pp.125,126)

It is nevertheless apparent that Religious Studies is becoming increasingly directed towards developing a critical understanding of the religious and moral dimensions of human experience and away from attempting to foster the claims of particular religions and standpoints but it is:

> ... self-defeating if it is only concerned with the study of 'the religious dimensions of human experience' and not with the realities which religious experience tries to grasp and respond to. (Newbigin, 1977, p.87)

There is a growing link between new Religious Studies and what has been variously described as 'education for international understanding', 'world studies', and 'multicultural education which takes British

---

* The production and implementation of an Agreed Syllabus is stipulated in the 1944 Education Act, which made the teaching of Religious Education in schools a statutory requirement.

society as its arena but which also has a global dimension'. The Centre for World Development Education emphasizes:

> those aspects [of Religious Studies] which bear on problems of social justice ... both what a religion teaches in theory and how its members behave in practice. (Davies *et al.*, 1979, p.12)

They suggest, therefore, that in a study of, say, Hinduism, topics such as the life of Gandhi, *ahimsa* (non-violence) and *satyagraha* (positive truth-force) contribute not only to increased knowledge but also to moral development. Richardson (1982) laments the omission from many Religious Studies syllabuses of issues pertaining to conflict and justice, and the lack of reference to colonialism and racism.

> We teach about the 5 K's of Sikhism more readily than about the massacre at Amritsar; about the gods and festivals of Hinduism more readily than... Kipling's infamous proposal that non-Europeans are 'half-devil and half-child'; about the prayers and mosques of Islam more readily than about petro-dollars or ... the second-class status of Muslim children in many European schools; about the synagogues, Sabbath and Bar Mitzvah more readily than about Shylock and Fagin, or the holocaust... To understand any particular religious community you have to understand the threats to its integrity and to its very existence which it has had to withstand from other human beings. (p.184)

Many Religious Studies teachers have found that, of all the world religions, Judaism offers the greatest supply of Conflict and Justice issues because antisemitism is so inextricably bound up with Jewish identity; Judaism therefore has immediate implications for the multi-cultural curriculum.

> The new religious education tries to stare facts in the face, and to present the living world in all its rich plurality. Sympathy, criticism, plurality - these are some of the slogans the teacher needs ... the new religious education is realistic, impartial, and sensitive. No indoctrination: only initiation into understanding, and so a resistance to the pressures ... of a conformist world. (Smart, 1972, pp.6,7)

2 Commitment, neutrality, and openness

> The traditional ambivalence between wanting students to understand and wanting them to believe must be ended. There is a difference between devotion and learning which must be respected once it is acknowledged. (Cole, 1972, p.23)

The tension between commitment and neutrality which characterizes many school subjects is especially poignant in Religious Studies because the content not only implies, it also contains value judgements. It is evident that new Religious Studies theoretically repudiates 'taking advantage of immature minds by using dishonest arguments' (Cole, 1978b, p.17) but, equally, the subjective nature of religious phenomena must 'stimulate value judgements' (Cole, 1978b, p.17), and not be allowed to lapse into 'woolly relativism' (Richardson, 1982). An additional complication consists in the teachers' and the examiners' own value positions in general, and religious commitment in particular - and the extent to which these can and should be reflected in classrooms and on examination syllabuses. Every life style requires some form and some degree of commitment, be it to a religious belief or to a non-religious outlook; even individuals convinced of their neutrality cannot avoid commitment to that persuasion; and it is essential, according to Hulmes (1979), that in Religious Studies opportunities are found for expression of religious commitment and the presentation of accurate information about religion. Mills (1976) offers three possible strategies: the mere statement of views; a bald presentation of 'facts' which permits free choice; or the provision of criteria to assist pupils in reaching a position of autonomy.

As a partial solution, we can say that objectivity and commitment are not mutually exclusive, and that there is a distinction between commitment to a particular life stance and enthusiasm about it as a subject of study. It could be argued that even for the purpose of presenting an objective, fair and balanced picture of stances for living (British Humanist Association, 1975), there is both a need and a challenge to produce a living model of personal commitment - precisely because, paradoxically, this is a vital component of all life-stances: Religious Studies is rendered a disservice if pupils are not given the opportunity to observe 'what it means to be committed'.

> Teaching religion is walking a tight-rope between commitment and openness. Some positive tension between the two is inseparable from anything that can properly be described as religious education. (Oliver, 1974, p.183)

The Standing Advisory Council on Religious Education (1980) suggests that if teachers recognize that every tradition has its value, children will respect the beliefs and practices of others 'because there are truths which they enshrine' (p.7) but, in the view of Attfield (1974), this is not to give actual encouragement to pupils to 'find a faith to live by':

> If the pupil moves on to faith, his journey must be without more support than would be given to a fellow pupil, moving in the opposite direction. (p.175)

In short, we must take a realistic view by recognizing that some form of commitment is both universal and also a matter of degree:

> If only the one hundred per cent believer can teach his faith, then little teaching takes place. (Woodward, 1973, p.24)

The human element in Religious Studies makes the negotiation of values and the open sharing of commitments both feasible and desirable.

3 Religion and response

> The alternative to inducting children into religious belief is the type of arid religious studies which is a mere naming of the parts, a kind of R.K. - or catechism - but on a world scale! Those who teach world religions must change not only their attitude but also their methods - that is, if they wish to present a religion to children as something which human

beings practise and believe in, and which helps them find a meaning in life, as opposed to presenting them with a theological system, something completely cerebral. (Cole, 1972, p.24; 1978d, p.49)

Whatever the new Religious Studies may become, it is clear that it cannot be based on pre-specified behavioural objectives.

While it may be questionable whether dominant/dependent relationships are more prevalent in Religious Studies than in any other subject, it is arguably more important in Religious Studies that there be an atmosphere conducive to free and open soul-searching, to mutual respect within the learning group, and to a full understanding of the dignity of being human, which all life-stances proclaim, and which multicultural education seeks to make a reality through the curriculum. On a positive note, one of the latest Agreed Syllabuses to be produced embraces the process model as intrinsic to Religious Studies:

> The more the child is able to articulate his experience, to pose questions, to probe experience and attempt to make sense of it, the more he will be able to understand and respond to religious questions and to the varieties of religious...expression. (Hampshire Education Authority, 1980, p.3)

Wood (1979) suggests further that form should be consonant with content if both are to have meaning:

> One of the saddest things to me about 'phenomenological', 'broad-based' approaches is the incredible dullness of style. Teachers who would never dream of using chalk-and-talk all the time in Biblical lessons seem to see nothing wrong with reading from a text-book or dictating notes in the area of world faiths. It's perhaps a truism to say that we all learn from the 'how' as well as from the 'what'. So teach Islam in a Muslim way. Be Jewish about your Judaism course. (pp.28f)

It is clear that the initial and in-service training of teachers is crucial in developing the abilities and fostering the attitudes necessary for such an approach.

Religious Studies which is broad in scope need not necessarily be uncreative or inhibit free enquiry. Indeed it should encourage pupils to engage in a variety of activities designed to stimulate them - cognitively and affectively - to ask questions, to analyse answers, to develop empathy, to collaborate with others in learning religion 'by discovery', to know themselves better.

> A pupil could hardly be thought to be religiously educated if he knew and understood a great deal about the life-stances of his neighbours, but was not conscious of what he himself believed. (Cox, 1975, p.133)

Table 1 summarizes curricular implications for Religious Studies which derive from an assimilationist, separatist or plural response to a society which is culturally diverse. Culture is variously defined but is generally considered to be a total material and non-material way of

Table 1: The response of Religious Studies to multiculturalism - a summary by the author

	ASSIMILATION	SEPARATISM	CULTURAL PLURALISM
Ideology	Total absorption of minority groups into mainstream; eradication of culture and religion; notion of normativeness	Encapsulation of minority culture; withdrawal of minority groups; self-help and separate provision	Minority groups' participation in just society; equal rights with majority; cultural status for all
Emphasis	On the majority	On minorities	On the majority and minorities; currently only an ideal
Attitude to religion	Deficit hypothesis: 'true' religion v. 'false' religion	Avoidance of conflict: religion a private matter for individuals and minority communities	Interactional approach: religious variability; diversity celebrated; mutual enrichment; notion of religion in evolution
Approach to Religious Studies	Neo-confessional	Confessional	Phenomenological
Curriculum content	Fossilized curriculum; high culture; narrowly ethnocentric	Ethnic studies; traditional scriptures	Curriculum permeated by openness to all cultural/religious sources. Awareness of stereotyping and religious prejudice
Organization of Religious Studies	Christian ideas permeate many school subjects (especially literature, history); evangelism as a process of socialization	Supplementary education: Cheder, Qu'ran schools etc.; religious maintenance for minorities in state schools	Mixed affiliation classrooms (all faiths and none); specialist Religious Studies teacher

life, containing elements of social organization, technology, and ideology - the latter being the most heavily emphasized in current literature. Ethnicity is that collective identity shared by members of a cultural minority who experience a sense of separateness from the majority. Patterns of relationship between ethnic minorities and the majority are diverse and can be placed on a continuum which ranges from assimilation to separatism. *Assimilation* is an integrative strategy (initiated by either the minority or the majority) which operates as though the society were monocultural by obliterating all features of cultural heterogeneity. To assimilate or not to assimilate is not always the prerogative of the minority and assimilation has the ambivalent property of high status and cultural annihilation. At the other end of the scale are differential responses, such as *separatism* which involves a recognition that distinctive ethnic groups can be accommodated only if accorded distinctive institutions and, ultimately, resources and power. *Cultural pluralism* recognizes the presence of distinctive groups but seeks to incorporate them within the mainstream culture on a coalitional basis; such a model is only feasible when issues on which groups differ are negotiable; mechanisms of negotiations are often formal and elaborate in attempting to promote both unity and diversity. Three fundamental propositions must be accepted: the universalization of human rights, the validity of cultural values and properties even when they depart from the majority, and a commitment to the resolution of social claims by mutual adjustment. Cultural pluralism thus represents a central position but, in a democratic society, does not constitute a compromise. It is the stand which best protects minorities and most enriches the majority; the benefit of cultural status is reciprocal. It is, as such, the most appropriate and valuable model for multicultural education in Britain today.

4 Summary and conclusions

New Religious Studies is characteristically phenomenological in its approach to life-stances, and has a dual function: to examine religious elements implicit in human experience, and to analyse critically but appreciatively, the explicit dimensions of religious phenomena. Both these approaches reveal that religion not only implies but also contains issues of knowledge and value, and this gives rise to the tension between commitment and neutrality, particularly as it impinges upon the roles of teacher and examiner: how to be honest and open with pupils without reverting to confessionalism and, conversely, how to remove purely subjective judgements without becoming a 'marking machine'? The answer conceivably lies in the extent to which pupils are positively encouraged to explore and express religious meanings under conditions conductive to cooperation and care for others. Multicultural Religious Studies can only be effective when 'unity within diversity' is manifest in the classroom, when teachers and learners join together in a process of self-development and self-discovery, and where there is a vision of goodness and truth.

II EXAMINING IN RELIGIOUS STUDIES: PRINCIPLES AND PROBLEMS

1 The relationship between the curriculum and examinations

> The influence of examinations on the teaching of the subject in secondary schools is enormous. (Hogbin, 1981, p.14)

The circular relationship between curriculum and examinations has long been recognized in Religious Studies, as indeed in most school subjects. It has been frequently used in the past in negative ways by, alternately, teachers or school-based curriculum innovators and examining boards: each would cite the constraints imposed by the other to explain or justify the inadequacy of their developments. Teachers of Religious Studies examination courses in secondary schools have frequently complained that, because of the time element, a crowded CSE or GCE O-level syllabus prevents them from extending the candidates' interests and abilities in new or exciting ways, while, on the other hand examining boards, subject officers, moderators and advisory panels in Religious Studies bemoan the innate conservatism of teachers which renders futile the promotion of more progressive syllabuses and examinations. This is no reason to despair. The exercise to formulate national criteria for the proposed single system of examining at 16+ has initiated a wider reappraisal by schools and boards - and this is a cause of hope.

To both parties is offered the possibility of an extensive overhaul. For the task which the Secretary of State has initiated, namely the formulation of national criteria for 16+ examinations, is so vast in scope and duration that it behoves those involved to devote themselves not merely to tinkering with a common system of examining at 16+, but also to a thorough reappraisal of the nature and purpose of Religious Studies at 16+, especially with regard to its multicultural aspects. There is, thus, the possibility of more positive reciprocity, not complaints and constraints but promotion and progress. At the very least, the expenditure of resources - both human and material - in the 16+ discussion warrants an outcome that has some creative curricular contribution to offer. This must not be wasted, for it is highly improbable that similar opportunities for radical revamping of syllabuses will, in the foreseeable future, be possible again - for reasons of financial stringency, as well as because of the need for a settled, stable pattern. It follows therefore that if the emerging 16+ Religious Studies syllabuses are to respond to our multicultural society they must do so *now*, and not be seen to reinforce and perpetuate for another generation of examiners and examinees, monocultural approaches and expectations.

A parallel might be drawn between examining boards and the country's legislative/judiciary: while Race Relations Acts in Britain do not of themselves put an end to, say, racial stereotyping or bigotry, they do exist to redress its worst offences and, in so doing, serve as society's statement about truth and equality. Similarly, if burgeoning Religious Studies examination syllabuses were to be affected by our multicultural society they would not immediately produce a plethora of teachers of world religions or of the 'religion and race' issues (and so on) but they would indicate that it is both acceptable and desirable for 16+ candidates to study non-Christian faiths, Christianity as perceived and practised by a variety of ethnic groups, and religious attitudes to race or religions. The syllabus might then be seen by teachers to be outlining more than fringe issues, and to be centrally proper to a course of study as well as being a valid focus for thought.

In any school, there is much confusion between the general and examination curriculum in Religious Studies, and a great disparity between what may be desirable as a Religious Studies curriculum for the 11-16 age range and what might be examinable at 16+.

> Arguments in favour of an essential core curriculum of knowledge and skills for the 11-16 stage of education also support the assessment of the effectiveness of the whole of that core curriculum through public examinations at 16+. (Marratt, 1981, p.8)

This is especially pertinent in the case of religious minority pupils who might need a form of Religious Studies which nurtures them in their faith but who could not be said to be religiously educated if that were the sum and substance of a 16+ syllabus and examination.

The gap can be closed only by communication and cooperation. Marratt argues that boards should reflect and embody the needs and goals of the schools. In order to facilitate this, it must be ensured that boards' 'proposals are realistic and workable and express rather than dictate the nature of education leading up to 16+.' (p.11)

2 Assessment difficulties: the problem of objectivity

> It is a fact that this country is full of talented people ... in the overwhelming majority of cases there is no piece of paper officially recognising [their] talents, and yet people find their status in life often stereotyped by these pieces of paper. (Mansell, 1981, p.30)

> Once one admits that some aims are fundamental to pupil assessment via the examination procedure teachers will begin to query how far age, background and other facts can be taken into account, so as not to disadvantage any pupil. (Marratt, 1981, p.10)

It is becoming almost standard practice for CSE boards - and, to a lesser extent GCE boards - to examine in Religious Studies partly by means of so-called objective tests (usually using a multiple-choice format) which are thought to provide an accurate assessment of pupils' knowledge of religious phenomena, e.g., rituals or texts. There are even some cases of objective tests being used to assess comprehension, interpretation, and evaluation. Greenwood and Marratt (1977) are convinced that there is a body of knowledge about religious beliefs and practices which candidates must acquire - and been seen to have acquired - if they are to be religiously educated. Objective testing is used so as 'not to discriminate religiously or morally between pupils but to encourage their full religious education.' (p.8)

The human mind may never perceive a thing as it really exists but there may yet be some agreement between people about the existence, nature, and appearance of purely physical phenomena. In the case of religious phenomena, however, no such empirical verification is possible. Those who seek to understand, say, worship must recognize that there is a disparity between the object of worship and the worshipper, as well as a disparity between the worshipper and the student. There are situations, too, when the worshipper and the student are one and the same; the matter might be rendered even more complex by the idea that individuals may share common perceptions of reality which transcend formal religious distinctions.

Many teachers maintain that there are no 'right' answers in Religious Studies, that objective tests are too blunt a measure for the sensitive, subtle areas of human life and that they only succeed in distorting the nature of religion in pupils' eyes. Thus, objective tests are severely criticized as gauges of subjective criteria. These difficulties may be less immediately apparent in other forms of Religious Studies assessment but they are no less serious; thus, the issue of objective testing highlights a central problem in assessing the subject.

Hogbin (1981) stresses the 'intrinsically controversial nature of religion' and 'legitimate and alternative interpretations of evidence' (p.20). It is not simply a matter of value pluralism - a problem which bedevils assessment in many subjects, but also of the unknown or unknowable nature of what is being taught, learned and, ultimately, examined.

The educational emphasis on process rather than product brings this point to a head, a point exemplified by the Schools Council Religious Education 16+ Sub-Committee's (1981) consciousness-raising list of questions regarding the formulation of objectives:

> Are the principles, procedures and skills those which the candidates can demonstrate under the conditions of assessment? Do the processes include evaluative principles, procedures and skills as well as descriptive, expository processes? (p.7)

The outstanding example of the unexaminable - and probably unenforceable - aim is:

> Every pupil should gain a knowledge of religion that enables him to achieve greater personal development and social competence. (p.i)

In this connection - and notwithstanding the need for academic rigour, Marratt (1981) acknowledges that the 16+ assessment may skirt around qualities such as empathy, understanding, and sensitivity because of the difficulties in devising procedures which assess them adequately and without subjectivity. It is, therefore, no understatement when Lealman (1981) writes that examination results in Religious Studies fail 'to reflect many skills and personal qualities. Nor do examinations show all that a student has studied.' (p.5)

3 Theoretical knowledge and practical experience

> The complexities of agreeing upon a common core of subject study is driving some working parties in the direction of skill-orientated rather than knowledge-possessed aims. (Marratt, 1981, p.10)

It was suggested by the Schools Council 16+ Sub-Committee that there should be a variety of examining modes - including practical tests which might reasonably be thought to be impossible, bizarre, maybe even a contradiction in terms. The popular image of religion is that it is impractical or, at the very least, non-practical, perhaps because it has been treated by teachers and examiners in the past simply as intellectual systems of belief, without recognizing its essentially personal and experiential aspects. However, religion is concerned with what people do - rituals and ethical actions - and not simply with what they think, with mere systems of dogma or patterns of reasons. It would follow, therefore, that Religious Studies must assume a practical, emotionally-involved experiential dimension - doing as well as thinking - and it seems feasible that a test be devised to measure experience of the ritual and moral dimensions of practised religion.

The practical nature of Religious Studies is demonstrated in the way it fits pupils for life, especially in the contemporary conditions of rapid social change. This is a point pursued by Hogbin (1981), who suggests that the qualities developed in Religious Studies - qualities which should be examined at 16+ - are of 'considerable relevance to employers since they are critical for success in any problem situation' (p.25). He has in mind the extension of process criteria to include the ways in which examinees handle tasks they have been assigned; for example, persistence and determination, management and organization, the willingness to recognize bias in oneself. He is fully aware that there are problems in assessing such attributes and tendencies, and he suggests that only the teacher can use process criteria in this case since such criteria require knowledge of the candidates over a period of time. Mansell (1981) strongly urges the use of student profiles to facilitate this.

4 Summary and conclusions

There are signs that in the relationships between Religious Studies teachers and examining boards, and between school curricula in Religious Studies and examination syllabuses, the boards and the examination syllabuses have dominated. There are equally strong signs of role liberation within this relationship, pointers to the influence 'upwards', indications of Religious Studies advisory panels to examining boards actively seeking out and attempting to fulfil teachers' expressed needs through teacher representation. The boards are in the position to offer a syllabus and an examination which teachers within schools can either take or leave. The teachers have the opportunity of imaginative developments to promote positive Religious Studies for a multicultural society - an opportunity never offered them before and unlikely to be offered again. But the monoculturalism - real or alleged - of classroom teachers is an inhibiting force. It is obviously undesirable to encourage a plethora of Mode IIIs which many would argue is a violation of the spirit of national criteria - and so reconciliatory work needs to be done. Some contentious issues are already emerging; at the centre is the question of Christianity as a compulsory element and this will be considered in Chapters IV and V.

Another area of potential contradiction is the extent to which an examination demands rigid, external criteria which, by their very nature, fail to meet such qualities as sensitivity, reflectiveness and responsiveness to value pluralism which Religious Studies might rightly purport to promote. More appropriate styles of examination are urged: possibly the use of student profiles, mixed-mode examining (a combination of school and board-based assessments), possibly some form of practical test, for example, conducting liturgy, wearing dress, preparing food, performing rituals, to reinforce the notion that religion is about what people *do* not just what they *think*.

III EXISTING 16+ PROVISION IN RELIGIOUS STUDIES: REVIEW AND REACTIONS

The current 16+ examination arrangements in the area of Religious Studies are many and varied: in fact, the differences and discontinuities are so vast as to render the subject in one geographical region almost unrecognizable in another. For the most part, the subject is known as Religious Studies (variously Religious Education, Scripture, and so on) but that in no way implies uniformity or conformity in aims, objectives or content of syllabuses or, indeed, of examination format.

There is also considerable diversity in the style and scope of examination syllabuses: some are lengthy documents offering specific points of information, others brief and stating general principles; some stipulate exact standards of study and presentation, others are open-ended and vague; some err on the side of too much guidance, others of too little.

A salient feature of almost all boards, however, is a marked disparity - verging on a dichotomy - between the stated aims and objectives and the stipulated content of the syllabus, and, also, between the syllabus and the examinations. In the majority of cases, the examination questions actually set from year to year do not reflect to the full the grandiose or idealistic aims given in the body of the syllabus; in particular, it can be noted that cognitive aims involving such processes and qualities as: individual thought, personal judgement, reasoned argument, and the like are not tested fully - perhaps never at all - in the examination papers. In some respects, they are actually incapable of being expressed in an examination answer by any but the most determined or defiant candidate. All of this means that an accurate and realistic review of the 16+ provisions in Religious Studies must take cognizance not only of the aims and objectives of a particular syllabus but also of the content and the question papers actually set. It also follows that any multicultural aims *must* be translated into syllabus content, and ultimately into classroom interaction and examination papers which offer scope for a multicultural perspective. They cannot be allowed to remain as indeterminate or unattainable ideals.

Notwithstanding this, there are clear indications that Religious Studies syllabuses have undergone fundamental changes over the last decade, and some new syllabuses have already been examined at 16+ while others are now in preparation for 1983 or 1984. Whereas formerly, Religious Studies syllabuses were exclusively Christian-oriented and mostly Bible-based, an easily discernible trend has been to include (as optional papers or sections) first what might broadly be described as 'religious responses to contemporary social questions', and also studies of non-Christian faiths. But there are one or two boards which have not made any such alterations and have no plans to do so, and several which have incorporated a response to contemporary social issues but not studies of world religions; AEB (see Appendix A for abbreviations of examining boards) produced an entirely different syllabus of alternative World Faiths. It must be stated quite categorically that there are also some boards which have religious - as opposed to educational - aims; which are concerned not so much with cognitive as with spiritual development (interpreted in an evangelical sense), and which would therefore not be in sympathy with the expansive aims of diversity, or multicultural awareness.

There are also instances where examination syllabuses lack internal consistency in aims; where, for example, one goal centres on Christian nurture, that is, on encouraging candidates to accept the full implications of the Christian faith; while another is concerned with promoting tolerance and celebrating a variety of religious approaches. The apparent conflict between two such aims might be explained by recent, partial changes of syllabus and examination. Piecemeal tinkering and modernization may mean that a board loses consistency between approach and purpose. It is hoped, therefore, that the 16+ national criteria exercise will produce a coherent pattern.

Kidd (1982) recounts that, at the Chichester conference held in December 1981, a representative of AEB cited statistics showing the solid support of teachers for the traditional Christianity syllabus (i.e., the Gospels in cycle), and also that 80 per cent of candidates choose Christianity and Modern Living as their second option. However, their Syllabus II, a multifaith alternative introduced in 1977 (mentioned above) had, by 1981, trebled its initial attraction of 335 candidates. Subject officers, moderators, and chief examiners of other boards also report a 'growing interest' and an 'increase in candidature' in the syllabuses covering world faiths.

A survey of existing 16+ Religious Studies possibilities (Mode I CSE and GCE O-level) reveals that there are primarily three aspects in which boards have responded to a multicultural society or through which such a response could be made; and these will be described and exemplified in turn, drawing on material made explicit by the boards through syllabuses and examination questions. For the sake of clarity and simplicity the three aspects may be referred to as: World religions, Prejudice and community relations, and Value pluralism.

1 World religions

World religions is examined, with the exception of the AEB World Faiths syllabus, in a separate optional paper/section and this is the most conspicuous of the aspects under review. Here the content is obvious and the attitudes and issues of value flow immediately from it. It will take one of two forms: typological wherein a religious system is studied (and therefore examined) in and of itself, although clearly not in its entirety; or thematic wherein the focus is a dimension of human experience or a common feature of organized religion, and this is viewed from the point of view of several systems (classically three or five). Both approaches have their strengths and weaknesses (which is probably why some boards offer a choice between the two). The typological sacrifices breadth for depth; the thematic depth for breadth. The typological permits an intense commitment to the study and individual sense of involvement; the thematic encourages an attitude of universal humanity and unity within diversity.

Whichever the approach, a World Religions paper theoretically avoids any culture-loading in religious terms. At the very least, it indicates that the world in general, and Britain in particular, is multifaith: that there are many faiths of equal validity and value. A criticism made of this approach is that Christianity features within the World Religions option (at least in the thematic approach) as well as being prominent in the traditional Christianity-based options. Against this, may be levelled the argument that a World Religions option which did not feature Christianity - and simply left it in its 'own' syllabus - would render it artificially prominent, and make it a special case.

The AEB O-level examination on world faiths aims to encourage:

> the sympathetic study of aspects of selected religious traditions with particular reference to their contemporary form;
>
> an awareness of the significance in each of the three faiths studied (selected from Christianity, Hinduism, Islam, Judaism, Sikhism) of three features: sacred buildings and places of pilgrimage, worship and festivals, scriptures.

In addition to an essay paper which carries 75 per cent of the marks, candidates are required to submit (for the remaining 25 per cent) a 3,000-4,000-word special study based on a single religion, chosen from: the family, birth, a ceremony of initiation, marriage or death. The objectives are clearly spelled out and weighted: factual knowledge (40 per cent); personal involvement (20 per cent); sensitivity and insight (20 per cent); logical and attractive presentation (20 per cent).

Men at Worship is one of the three options which Cambridge candidates may offer in conjunction with a New Testament O-level examination. It consists of coursework and a written paper which covers four thematic areas: rites of initiation, places of worship, occasions of worship, how men worship. The aims are bold: 'to promote an understanding of some of the beliefs and practices of people of different faiths in a pluralistic society. Emphasis should be placed on the practice rather than the historic development of Hinduism, Buddhism, Judaism, Christianity, Islam and Sikhism.'

Both a thematic and a limited typological approach are available in the World Faiths option of London's O-level examination: candidates may choose to study Judaism (written and oral law, beliefs, ethical behaviour, the sabbath: festivals and fasts, public and private practices) or Islam (the five pillars, Muslim festivals, Jihad, the mosque, social practices and institutions) or Aspects of Five World Faiths (namely Christianity, Hinduism, Islam, Judaism, Sikhism). The aspects involve marriage and funeral customs, the scriptures, places of worship, festivals and ceremonies. Each World Religions option is taken in conjunction with one of the other options, which include Biblical sections as well as Personal and Social Relationships and Problems; an exclusive study of Christianity is therefore not mandatory. There are no aims peculiar to the World Religions section but, in general, the syllabus is designed to enable pupils:

(i) to study ... the material which forms the basis of religious knowledge including the relevant historical background, documents, practices;

(ii) to be aware of, formulate and evaluate differing interpretations of that material;

(iii) to express with honesty their own understanding of the material studied and to consider its significance;

(iv) to consider generally the nature of religion and to develop religious insight and thought.

The Christian's Encounter with Other Faiths forms one-third of The Attitude and Responsibility of the Christian to the World Community part of Alseb's examination in Religious Studies; while it is quite clear that this entails a Christo-centric approach, there is nevertheless an element of openness and wider awareness: indeed the contents specify some study of Judaism, Islam, Hinduism and 'points of contact between these world religions and Christianity particularly the first two' and includes 'World Council of Churches dialogue in this area'.

Like London, EA presents both typological and thematic opportunities. Its northern-based syllabus stipulates *one* Biblical section but the second might be Multifaith World, wherein three systems including Christianity must be chosen from seven which comprise Hinduism, Buddhism, Judaism, Christianity, Islam, Sikhism, and - uniquely - Humanism. The belief system is dealt with according to, its origins wherever applicable, teachings, sacred book(s), festivals, worship and holy places, way of life, and some outstanding personalities. In EA (South), World Religions exists as one of five sections of which candidates must offer two: they must study the origins, beliefs and practices of two religions chosen from Hinduism, Judaism, Christianity, Islam, Sikhism. A highly imaginative, 'anthropological' section of this same board's syllabus is entitled Religion - a Thematic Approach and is based on three categories of concepts which are felt to be central to the understanding of the nature of religion: 'religion in tribal cultures ... the expression of religion in language, acts and objects ... faith and behaviour'.

Certain aspects of non-Christian religions are featured in the four EM options of which candidates must chose one in addition to the compulsory unit on the life of Jesus. For example, 'The Role of Religion within the Family and Community' incorporates Bar Mitzvah, Hindu thread, living on a Kibbutz, and a Buddhist view of suffering. The Worship option is much more comprehensive and draws from a wide range of examples taken from the 'big five'.

LR's projected Syllabus C for 1983 requires an introductory study of five religions: Christianity, Hinduism, Islam, Judaism and Sikhism. The examination seeks to assess the extent to which the candidates are able to identify, describe and explain historical and geographical background; places of worship; its 'authentic media': writings, places, and people; festivals and rites of passage.

The only non-Christian religion available for study as an option with NR is Islam (it should be noted here that a paper in the Synoptic

Gospels - Matthew, Mark and Luke - is compulsory). 'The purpose of this course is to enable the pupil to understand what it means to be a Muslim.' It addresses itself to such controversial issues as the Role of Women, Forces for Change - Education, Work and Nationalism, and A Case Study of *One* Country with a Strong Islamic Tradition.

The NW Syllabus B has one option which aims to 'involve pupils in the examination and understanding of religious truth and to evaluate the part played by religion in human experience.' It combines the typological and thematic and looks especially at 'living among people of other faiths' and the value of religion to individuals and communities, 'the part religion can play in the crises of human life'.

The Life and Teaching of Jesus Christ is compulsory for candidates sitting the SE examination. They must additionally produce a 2,000-word piece of coursework: this can be within World Religions and, if so, must be an introductory study of two faiths - one Western and one Eastern. Another possibility is A Personal Study, which involves original investigation. Suggested topics include the Religious Significance of Food and the London Central Mosque in Regent's Park.

SR is unusual in having devised an alternative syllabus which demands seven projects which carry 60 per cent of the final mark: one must be devoted to the teaching of Christ, three to Christian moral principles, two should be concerned with the study of a major world religion or the life of a great religious person (not necessarily Christian); the last is a free choice. Similarly, a study leading to the understanding of a religion other than Christianity 'is possible as a piece of course work for the other two alternative syllabuses'.

In SW's syllabus, the Life and Teaching of Jesus Christ is compulsory but it can be paired with Aspects of Three World Religions - the novel combination of Judaism, Islam, and Sikhism. The overall aim is to relate religious understanding to everyday life.

The WM Syllabus A permits a special study (in addition to the Life and Teaching of Jesus Christ) on topics specified by the board, namely An Individual's Response to God or Symbols of Religion (1983), and A Religious Community or Rites of Passage (1984). Alternatively, 'to encourage a sympathetic understanding of three major faiths and the beliefs, hopes and aspirations of the adherents' a World Religions paper is offered: this has an interesting section on 'the position of the religion within the United Kingdom: problems; culture clash; charitable works; religion as a link for migrants.' Christianity is obligatory and must be combined with two other religions chosen from: Hinduism, Islam, Judaism or Sikhism.

Again, in WYL's syllabus, the major monotheistic religions (defined as Judaism, Christianity and Islam) can be chosen to accompany the compulsory Life and Teaching of Christ. It is 'to be essentially seen as a quest for knowledge and understanding... Teachers and pupils should travel together over this new ground of World Religions and, whilst keeping to the main direction indicated by the syllabus, they should feel free to explore at least some of the discoveries which attract their special attention. The teaching should not consist of the presentation of a mass of unrelated facts [but] should enable pupils to acquire some insight into the meaning and influence that [the main themes and principles] have in the lives of those who believe in them.'

Buddhism, Judaism, and Islam seldom appear together as alternatives but under World Religions they combine to form a theme, developed in Northern Ireland in 1980, which could form half the syllabus (the other half is to be Biblical knowledge). It is to be an in-depth study of one of the three, and the aims are those of the rest of the examination: 'knowledge, understanding the religious dimension of the topics studied, responsible and informed judgements'.

2 Prejudice and community relations

This is a blanket term to cover those areas of facts and issues concerned with questions of ethnicity, bias and stereotyping, human rights, and race relations. Most Religious Studies examinations feature these concerns, if only obliquely, but the limitations (from the standpoint of assessment in a multicultural society) are that they only appear in optional sections and that these have a predominantly Christian background and basis. In many cases they can only be taken in addition to The Life and Teaching of Jesus whereas they could equally complement other areas of the syllabus, particularly World Religions. The unwitting impression is given that only Christianity is concerned with race relations; other religions, it is implied, are wrapped up in ritual and bound by belief. No board as yet has a wide spectrum of religious traditions to draw upon in this domain, and only a few explicitly allow non-Christian sources in candidates' contributions; furthermore, it is lamentable that this topic is sometimes presented negatively, as a problem and source of stress, instead of in a positive light, emphasizing its enriching and ennobling qualities. There are even occasions where emphasis on Christian theoretical beliefs about race actually confirms ignorance and bigotry. In particular, antisemitism is sometimes fuelled by questions on the teaching of Jesus.

If Religious Studies is to develop fully along multicultural lines, this is clearly an area in need of expansion and development: it is fortunate that such an alteration would be fairly straightforward to effect and, given the will to change, a great deal could be accomplished with relatively little effort: without adjusting the overall structure of these sections, they could fill a wider need by the inclusion of non-Christian material on race relations. The examples from board syllabuses and examination papers which follow illustrate the present and potential coverage of these issues.

Apart from AEB's World Faiths syllabus, there is an option, The Relevance of Christianity to Contemporary Living, which covers 'The different forms of prejudice, notably racial, colour, social and religious prejudices. The factors which encourage prejudice should be considered together with ideas of what the Christian's response to prejudice should be. Some consideration should also be given to movements and organisations which are working to counter prejudice and to encourage unity.'

> H.G. Wells said that there was 'no more evil thing' than race prejudice. Why would a Christian consider race prejudice 'evil'? Explain why you agree or disagree with H.G. Wells

that there is 'no more evil thing' than race prejudice. (AEB, November 1981; 055/2, Section D, 36)

The World Council of Churches regularly gives a grant of money to help the victims of racism in their struggle for liberation. What arguments can be presented for and against this action? In your answer show that you understand the phrases 'victims of racism' and 'struggle for liberation'. (AEB, June 1982, 055/2, Section B(3), 22)

The Cambridge syllabus suggests that Martin Luther King is one of those who has 'undertaken [work] in the face of suffering'. Furthermore, in The Church and Society candidates are required to study 'the changing role of Christian missionaries in countries overseas ... the Church in a multifaith society'.

Should the presence of people of different faiths (e.g., Hindu, Sikh, Moslem) in Britain affect the kind of religious education that is provided in schools? What form of religious education do you think should be provided in schools today? (Cambridge, June 1981, 2042/5, 4)

Christian responsibility as examined by JMB involves a consideration of 'relationships under stress: attitudes towards people of other religions, races, colours or classes; crime and punishment; divorce.' The concessional (see page 41) Catholic paper Christian Life and Belief also includes the topic 'Attitudes towards peoples of other religions, races, colours, or classes. Religious factors which encourage prejudice'.

'When an alien settles in your land, you shall not oppress him. He shall be treated as a native born among you.'

(a) Suggest *three* difficulties which may arise in applying teaching from Deuteronomy in this country today.

(b) Consider what might be done to overcome these difficulties by

(i) the state
(ii) the churches
(iii) individuals

(JMB, June 1982, A, 7)

In problems of national and international relationships, including race and prejudice, certain Biblical passages are specified for study in London's optional Personal and Social Relationships and Problems. However, reference to other religious literature is permitted, and, indeed, candidates are expected to show a knowledge of the religious and/or non-religious facts and factors on which people's judgements are based.

'Racial prejudice presents society with serious problems.' What religious or ethical approach would you recommend as a solution? (London, January 1982, Section 6, 46)

It has been said that racial prejudice grows out of poor religious and moral teaching. Do you agree with this? Give careful reasons for your answers. (London, June 1982, Section 6, 44)

Race is a part of Oxford's paper, The Application of some Biblical Principles to Modern Life, representing 'a variety of beliefs on subjects relating to human experience'. Biblical passages are suggested as a basis of 'the changing attitudes today towards some Christian beliefs and practices'.

How would you counter racial prejudice by reference to the Old and New Testaments? Describe the work of any person who has sought to improve race relations today. (Oxford, summer 1981, 2841/7,9)

Religious Responsibility is a possible choice for SUJB's candidates and it entails a study of 'Stresses in Society: conflicts of religion, race, colour and class'.

Most of Britain has been a multi-racial society for a thousand years but, with the exception of the Jewish faith, it has not been multi-religious. What special problems does this pose in society in general and in school? (SUJB, June 1982, 2050, Section C, 25)

Similarly, in Part II of the Alseb syllabus projected for 1984, 'the attitude and responsibility of a Christian to family, friends, community, and authority' involves 'class and race relations - prejudice and intolerance, sexism.'

(a) It is sometimes said that we are all born equal. Give illustrations to show that this may not always be true.

(b) What kinds of people in your own school or your own district are not treated 'equally'? Why is this?

(c) In spite of all this, why do Christians still insist that we are all equal? In what ways can this be true, and how can it be applied to everyday life? (Alseb, May 1982, Section B, Part 2, 7)

Problems of relationships and prejudice - race, class, sex, mental illness feature in EA (North)'s Christianity and Modern Life, and community relations, including racial and class prejudice, apartheid, integration and racism in EA (South)'s Christianity in Practice: Living in Today's World.

(a) What is the meaning of prejudice?

(b) Give an example from the Bible condemning prejudice.

(c) Suggest ways in which Christians can work to overcome *three* types of prejudice in modern society. (EA (North), May 1981, Paper II, F26)

Community Relations

(a) Describe some of the attempts which have been made in recent years to ensure racial equality in Britain.

(b) What are the main reasons for the tension which still exists between different ethnic groups?

(c) What guidance can a Christian find in the New Testament on these problems? (EA (South), May 1981, B12)

A less common context is the Problem of Suffering in which EM examines 'religious discrimination (i) against Jews, (ii) against Christians in Communist countries, (iii) secular attitudes towards religious believers ... [and] racial discrimination in Britain'.

When young immigrants from Asia or the West Indies come to Britain, what differences might they find between the family life of this country and that of the country from which they came? (EM, May 1980, Paper 2, Theme 1, Part 2,2)

LR's newly devised Syllabus B contains a section on Community Responsibility, part of which consists of 'Prejudice and Discrimination - the reasons for prejudice, Racial and Religious Intolerance, The Rights of Minorities' and 'Justice and Freedom - civil and religious liberties'.

Prejudice

(a) What is the teaching in the New Testament about racial prejudice?

(b) What can we do in our own community to carry out the ideas of Conrad Hunte (the West Indian cricketer) who hoped that many races could learn to live and work together? What difficulties do you think will arise? (LR, June 1982, 200000/201000/1, Part B, Section 2, 29)

NW's revised syllabus includes, within one optional section, Living Among People of Other Faiths, and, within another, Working for Human Rights. Here Martin Luther King and Trevor Huddleston are recommended for study. Christianity and Race Relations is suggested as a possible topic for projects done by pupils.

(a) Describe three causes of racial prejudice in Britain today.

(b) Comment on the provisions which have been made or should be made to help people from other countries to settle in Britain.

(c) In Mark 7, verses 24-30, we read of a meeting between Jesus and a Syro-Phoenician woman. Explain their conversation.

(NW, May 1980, Syllabus A, Paper 2, Section D, 33)

SE examines, in its compulsory section, Class Distinction and Race Relations - (i) Jesus shows his love for people of all nations, (ii) Jesus shows his love for social outcasts; this is to be applied to modern life in terms of 'Who is my neighbour? Prejudice, discrimination and persecution. Outcasts and minority groups'.

(a) Relate the conversation between Jesus and the Syro-Phoenician woman.

(b) Explain what is meant by (i) prejudice, (ii) discrimination, giving an example in each case.

(c) In what ways are parents able to influence the attitudes of their children? (SE, May 1982, Paper 2, 4A)

SR suggests Colour and Racial Prejudice as ways in which the life and teaching of Jesus might be applied to Contemporary Problems and Situations in the World. Additionally, the Christian Living examination paper addresses itself, with Biblical references, to 'Prejudice, personal and racial', while the coursework includes studying Bishop Trevor Huddleston and Martin Luther King.

(a) Look up John 9, verses 1 to 34. Comment on the personal prejudice shown in this story.

(b) Make a list of *four* different kinds of prejudice.

(c) Select *two* examples from your list and say what the Christian attitude should be in each case. (SR, May 1982, Alternative 2, Section B, 4)

Integration of Immigrants

Either:

(a) (i) What do you think is meant by 'integration'?

(ii) Do you think that Christianity has a contribution to make in the integration of immigrants?

Give your reasons.

Or:

(b) (i) Why do many immigrants tend to live in their own group?

(ii) Show how Christian principles can be involved both for and against integration. (SR, May 1982, Alternative 3, Section 2, 3)

If SW candidates opt for Christian Belief and Action, they will be studying 'the meaning of prejudice and discrimination. Class, sex, race, colour, religion. Positive responses to discrimination'.

(a) State *four* ways in which people sometimes think they are better than others.

(b) State briefly the part *each* of the following plays in the development of prejudice: (i) fear, (ii) ignorance, (iii) insecurity.

(c) What can we learn from the teaching of any *one* major religious leader that would help to remove barriers that exist between people?

(d) The Universal Declaration of Human Rights states that 'All human beings are born free and equal in dignity and rights'. What can be done to make this more of a reality (i) by governments and organisations, and (ii) by you? (SW, May 1982, Paper II, 3)

The WM syllabus Christianity and Life includes 'Prejudice and concern for others ... the causes of prejudice - social customs - fear - ignorance - herd instinct - different types of prejudice - colour - class-minority groups - gypsies - hippies - homosexuals - the removal of prejudice - harmony - racial purity, racial integration - Jesus and other races ... Race Discrimination Act; The Brotherhood of Man - nationalism - internationalism'. Elsewhere Dietrich Bonhoeffer and Martin Luther King are suggested as topics.

(a) A Christian who thinks of God as 'Father' must also think of all men as being his 'brothers'. What does the 'Brotherhood of Man' mean?

(b) (i) Why is the phrase 'The Third World' used to describe certain countries?

(ii) Write down *four* characteristics which Third World countries share.

(c) During a period of economic difficulties at home, should the United Kingdom continue to give aid to Third World countries? Give reasons for your answer. You may refer to Biblical passages you have studied. (WM, June 1982, Paper IIA, 6)

New Testament references are supplied for Race Prejudice and Class Distinction which is part of the topic 'Christian Ethics in Modern Society', an optional theme with WYL.

(a) Describe the conditions which faced Albert Schweitzer and his wife on their arrival in Lambarene.

(b) Where did Albert Schweitzer site his hospital and organise his 'hospital'?

(c) As Albert Schweitzer became famous, what opinions were expressed about him? Were these opinions always fair?

(WYL, May 1980, Paper II, Theme B, Section 3, 33)

Similarly Human Relationships with Other Races forms part of YR's Christianity and Life.

<u>Prejudice</u>

Unfortunately, prejudice on grounds of sex, race, class, colour or religion has long existed in the world and remains a problem today.

(a) In Bible times, women were very much 'second class citizens', but Jesus showed far more concern for their rights than did most people of this day. Name two separate incidents/parables which illustrate this statement.

(b) Why were people like Matthew and Zaccheus despised?

(c) Which race was hated by the Jews in Jesus' time? (In Old Testament times this race had been refused entry to the Temple at Jerusalem and so had built their own rival temple at Mount Gerizim.)

(d) Psalm 137 (verse 1 of which was Top of the Pops two years ago) tells of the Jewish attitude to their enemies while in captivity and exile.

(i) Verses 7-9 are typical of the Jewish attitude to their enemy. Express this attitude in your own words.

(ii) What did Jesus say in the Sermon on the Mount about attitudes to enemies?

(iii) Name an occasion when Jesus put this teaching into practice.

(e) Prejudice even extended to animals. The unclean animal in the gospels is the pig.

In which parable is pig-feeding the occupation of a man who has ruined his life?

(f) (i) Which world leader persecuted the Jews in the 1930's and 1940's?

(ii) Outline *three* examples of racial prejudice in the world today.

(iii) Criticise racial prejudice from a Christian point of view. (YR, June 1980, Paper 2, Section A, 4)

The NI syllabus refers to 'God and my neighbour: the Challenge of world problems .... prejudice and intolerance in group relations - sex, race, colour, religion ... problems of immigration, segregation and integration'.

Comment on the view that certain developments in the programme to combat racism have severely damaged the World Council of Churches. (NI, O level, 1982, Theme II, 62)

(a) What are the most common causes of racial and religious prejudices?

(b) What arguments would you use in an attempt to overcome such prejudice? (NI, O level, 1982, Theme 10, 58)

(a) You are helping with a door-to-door collection for Christian Aid or Trocaire when someone says 'I don't see why I should have to help them. What have they ever done for me?'

How might a Christian reply to this criticism? Give *two* main points in your answer.

(b) Write a paragraph on each of the following:

(i) Describe an incident when Jesus overcame *racial* prejudice.

(ii) Describe an incident when Jesus overcame *social* prejudice.

(c) Suggest *four* points St. Paul might make on the subject of prejudice if he was to write to the Christians in Northern Ireland today. (NI, CSE, 1982, Paper IIB, 7)

3 Value pluralism

> Questions about values are not susceptible to clear-cut or hard and fast solutions; in fact ... they are questions to which a number of different solutions can be proposed with equal justification and validity. (Kelly, 1980a, p.11)

Value pluralism is an attitude to thought and culture which accepts the differences between individual or group basic moral views and distinctions between individuals' and groups' perceptions of reality, and agrees to accommodate the consequences of such differences. To accept value pluralism is to acknowledge, first, that people differ not only in dress, personal habits, and the like, but also in more fundamental questions of belief, behaviour, and belonging; and second, that no one ethical code or set of religious beliefs is better than another in any absolute sense. '"Different" means "different": it does not mean better than or worse than.' (Rivlin, 1973, p.vii)

Value pluralism is conceivably the most important area to develop in terms of multicultural assessment yet it is undoubtedly the most inaccessible of all the desirable qualities, and the most difficult to examine. Boards may be at a loss as to how far they can allow the candidates the inevitable subjectivity that is involved, for so much depends on what constitutes, and what can be construed as, a valid argument or sufficient reason. Equally, it is impossible to assess the extent to which a board might really embody its stated ideal of openness and acceptance. It is much more a matter of professional judgement than it is an exact science.

There are two sources of value pluralism to bear in mind: firstly, the perceptions, understandings, and attitudes which candidates, individually and collectively, bring to bear on the examination, and, secondly, the beliefs and practices which exist as the body of knowledge that forms the basis of Religious Studies.

A variant on value pluralism might be described as concessionalism: that is, a basically monocultural or monoreligious approach which tolerates deviation from the norm. To fill this need some boards provide special examinations for Roman Catholic and Jewish candidates; any other group regarded as distinctive might also similarly be catered for. Concessionalism may well stem from a multicultural perspective on the part of those who offer or permit it (the boards); but often reflects an entrenched and reinforced monoculturalism on the part of those who demand or accept it (the schools and candidates). Accordingly, denominational papers have not been taken as the writer's brief because the set of issues involved in them differs from those involved in broad-based, multifaith Religious Studies examinations. Denominational papers present *one* aspect of examination with a specific cultural emphasis but some are inevitably so partisan that it is questionable whether they can fulfil the same aims as 'objective' examinations in Religious Studies: this is because they generally purport primarily to confirm candidates in their own religious culture and not to encourage in them an awareness of other religious cultures. If denominational examinations are to continue, the breadth of viewpoint might be served by extending the choice to incorporate all minority religions and by making the approach explicit in the title of the examinations. Rastafarianism - so badly neglected until now - warrants special emphasis in the future and is considered briefly by the author in Chapter V.

Appendix C, a CSE Mode II syllabus on Islam, is an example of a proposed denominational syllabus along these lines: it is not typically Muslim and is open to all candidates 'of all faiths and none'. The syllabus is an attempt to bring a seemingly denominational paper within the orbit of Religious Studies in terms of aims and objectives; but the acceptability to the Muslim Community of the syllabus - which encourages criticism and which need not necessarily be taught by a Muslim - is questionable.

Value pluralism really amounts to much more than a board's indifference to the version of the Bible from which a candidate chooses to quote; it is a question of permitting - even encouraging and expecting - a variety of, say, moral views or Biblical interpretations; indeed, the subject matter is immaterial: what is significant is the willingness to welcome self-determination and self-definition. Value pluralism has been defined in various ways:

> Critical but sympathetic handling of the subject matter (i.e., not showing blind acceptance nor unfeeling prejudice);
>
> knowledge of religious ideas and developments ... and of the different interpretations of these;
>
> candidates ... should not think that Christianity provides a set of unequivocal answers which merely need to be applied;
>
> the variety of religious experience. (AEB)

> Other attitudes - ancient and modern;
>
> different parts in a pluralistic society. (Cambridge)

> Success in the examination will in no way depend upon a candidate's religious beliefs or lack of them;
>
> evaluation and ability to express reasoned views;
>
> awareness of different interpretations of facts. (JMB)

> [Candidates should] express with honesty their own understanding of the material studied;
>
> Candidates must illustrate their answers and arguments by ... evidence. (London)

> Different forms of belief: scientific, moral and religious ... Beliefs about the value of human life and the dimensions of a person ... Beliefs about the purpose of life;
>
> The moral 'codes' in the major belief systems. (EA, South)

> ... religious and non-religious homes - a personal evaluation;
>
> why is there suffering? - a study of Christian and Buddhist views (EM)

[Candidates should] express their own understanding and attitudes towards the topics studied;

a sympathetic understanding of religious beliefs and practices. (LR)

It is not intended to examine personal belief ...

the religious influences and principles, whether explicit or implicit, should be emphasised. (SE)

No candidate will be penalised for expression of any opinion or point of view which is given reasoned support. (SR)

Varying interpretations of Christian teaching;

the Board accepts as a definition of religion that religion is man's search for and his relationship with a god;

The various ways in which man expresses his spiritual life. (WM)

It is not intended to examine a pupil's personal religious life. (YR)

Contemporary approaches to belief; theism - rational grounds for belief; atheism - rational rejection of God to include the critiques of Marx and Freud; indifference; fideism; religious experience; agnosticism.

Science and religion as ways of interpreting experience. Proof in religion and science. (NI)

4 Scotland

A brave and inspired decision has been made by Scotland to introduce a syllabus and examination in Religious Studies at the ordinary grade from 1984. Such a development must be warmly welcomed by all interested in multicultural education and in a process model of the curriculum. Although not directly affected by the 16+ proposals over the border, the Scottish programme is nevertheless a model of what can be achieved with determination, enlightenment, and courage.

The heart of the syllabus is its concern with religious phenomena and the human experiences from which they arise; questions posed - and answers proposed - by religions on the meaning of existence, and beliefs and behaviour resulting from growth and self-discovery. As to the content, there is a compulsory Christian core and an equally weighted component on Hinduism, Islam or Judaism. This, of itself, is perhaps unexceptional and unexceptionable but it is combined with a school-assessed original report on an aspect of one or more stances for living and is examined through differentiated questions structured on an incline of difficulty and based on resources supplied to the candidates, so as to reduce their reliance on factual recall and encourage speculation. For example, in the specimen paper, one of the questions on Christianity is stimulated by copies of Christmas cards; the questions are about the religious symbolism in the cards and the significance that Christmas has for individual Christians. A black line drawing of Krishna prompts 'Hindu Gods and Goddesses are often shown with many arms. Why is this so?' A comprehension test after a passage on Islam runs: 'How might this knowledge [about Mohammad's childhood] help your understanding of Mohammad's saying that "every child is born with a Muslim heart"?' A passage from the Bible (II Samuel 7:8-12) gives rise to: 'In your opinion, how far does the modern Jewish State of Israel express traditional Jewish religious ideals?'

5 Summary and conclusions

It is hoped that the 16+ national criteria exercise, and the re-thinking which it entails, will bring with it a certain sense of coherence and consistency - qualities which have been absent from Religious Studies syllabuses and examination papers in the past.

The World Religions approach to Religious Studies tends to include Christianity both in its thematic and its typological styles. Criticisms are sometimes voiced against boards which allow Christianity to 'creep into' World Religions sections of syllabuses, as Christianity is already dominant by virtue of its occupation of traditional sections; but this dominance might seem to be emphasized if it enjoys this special role without being included in other sections. There is obviously, therefore, a case to be made for the inclusion of Christianity alongside Sikhism and so on.

The areas of syllabuses concerned with religious responses to race relations are firmly located in the Christian tradition, which implies that only Christianity has anything to offer. There is a strong reason to use, say, the literature from several systems to find positive ways of approaching human diversity.

The nub of the matter is the extent to which value pluralism is taken seriously. It can be remarked that differences in religion are *different* from other kinds of human differences: there is a nutritional, gastronomic and cultural difference between eating chappattis and eating chips but such differences are unlikely to be of the same earth-shattering importance as believing in Krishna or Christ - a matter of ultimacy. Value pluralism can only blossom where there are issues of ultimate concern and competing claims for truth, but, paradoxically, it is these that make it so difficult a challenge.

Those examining boards which have latterly become more 'progressive' have tended to do so by adding to their syllabuses new options - gently, tentatively breaking their way in and not making anything compulsory until it has first been optional. They have, at the same time, retained their more traditional elements. While this has rendered syllabuses bulky and unwieldy, it does mean that candidates have a wider choice.

IV CURRENT PROPOSALS FOR RELIGIOUS STUDIES AT 16+: CRITERIA AND CRITICISMS

> Should syllabuses in Religious Studies not only preserve the study of Christianity but also make it compulsory for candidates to study one other major world religion?
> (Joint 16+ Council, 1982)

There is perhaps an analogy here: those in favour of retaining educational selection at 11+ can often be heard to mourn the passing of the grammar school: 'It was a good place. It worked well. It was a success - what a pity to close it down. Quite wrong!' When presented with the arguments for a comprehensive system of secondary schooling, they are perhaps convinced of the case for equity or equality but wonder why the two systems cannot exist side by side. Clearly, there is a basic failure here to see that the existence and provision of one undermines the existence of the other.

So it is with the question of a compulsory core in 16+ Religious Studies: there are those who argue for either a Christianity core or a totally Christianity-based syllabus 'for those who want it' (they usually mean themselves). They continue to suggest that World Religions or Religious Responses to Society might coexist with it, without perceiving the deleterious effect of one upon the other. There can be no parity of esteem in the World Religious component if one of them is 'creamed off' for special treatment and extra recognition.

Just as the bishops in the House of Lords will always (according to the quip) vote against sin, so the aims of the GCE and CSE Boards' Joint Council Draft 16+ National Criteria for Religious Studies will - with one or two notable exceptions - receive broad general assent from those parties with a legitimate interest. Some might want to add certain aims - especially confessional ones - but it is unlikely that any would be struck off. The real issue at stake is, interestingly, the one most pertinent to the notion of assessment in a multicultural society, namely, whether there should be a common core and, if so, whether it should be Christian and in what form.

As a preliminary draft in January 1982, the Joint Council's 16+ Religious Studies Working Party recommended a common core in which 'candidates should be assessed on a study of the religion which is a fundamental element in the culture of this country.'* The Schools Council Religious Education 16+ Sub-committee also urged that this 'national system of examination ... reflect the common basis of the mainstream religious and cultural tradition of the United Kingdom.'

---

* See p.48 for 'final' draft details.

There are several cogent counter-arguments. First, cultural acclimatization is not one of Religious Studies' functions and, at any rate, it had curiously not been forwarded as an aim by either the Joint Council Working Party or the Schools Council Sub-committee; secondly, if cultural acclimatization *is* desired, then atheistic humanism or unthinking secularism are debatably more apt; thirdly, world awareness is arguably more important than British awareness; and, if a single religious tradition or life-stance were chosen as a vehicle for Religious Studies as such, the purpose might better be served by Buddhism - on the grounds that it is the most popular - or Islam - because it is the fastest growing in the world; fourthly, the position of religious minority pupils in Britain must be appreciated: not only would a Christian common core not offer parity of esteem, but the minority candidate - indeed any non-Christian - might suffer a severe disadvantage in relation to Christians, whatever were combined with the core. If we have a multicultural society in the forefront of our minds, we must be careful - at the very least - not to reinforce any negative discrimination. It is quite indefensible to impose on committed members of other communities an obligatory study of Christianity especially if they have been 'saturated' with a course on Christianity for five years of secondary education and possibly six years of primary education before that, as is the case in most British schools, since Religious Education is still a compulsory subject in the curriculum. It is one thing to want to ensure that all school pupils have an understanding and appreciation of the Christian tradition and its impact on world history and British culture, but quite another to make it obligatory in an optional public examination course. In any event Religious Studies is about religion, not about British society - or even society at all, and the subject is distorted when it is discussed as though it existed solely as a vehicle for civic initiation. The fundamental question Religious Studies addresses itself to is What is religion?; not, What is Britain like?

The Joint Council Religious Studies Working Party in its January 1982 preliminary draft, further proposed that there be a 'second component comprising either (i) a study of a major world religion other than Christianity; or (ii) a further study of Christianity different from the common core; or (iii) a selected aspect of religious faith and practice.' It follows, therefore, that candidates could offer *two* Christian components and nothing else: this would be incompatible with the title 'Religious Studies', and with some of the intentions expressed by the Working Party in its introduction. There would be no encouragement to develop a sense of diversity, empathy or the ability to 'stand in another's shoes'.

The Schools Council Religious Education 16+ Sub-committee's draft proposal is slightly closer to achieving a multicultural aim in that it requires 'a study of a second religion' suggesting that:

> Christianity [should] be studied in a broader context ... it should not have a privileged status in academic terms, and full justice [should] be done to the conviction that the study of religion especially when undertaken in a multi-faith society, should involve more than the study of one religion. (p.1)

Thus the Schools Council's 16+ Sub-committee draft rules out the possibility of candidates studying only one tradition as well as what they dismiss and disparage as 'the Cook's Tour approach' (although they neglect to explain why they find this educationally undesirable). They assume that by treating candidates in the same way, they are being equally fair; but 'same' and 'equal' are different because minority pupils have less choice. If they wish to study their own religion, they cannot also choose which other religion they wish to offer for examination; it is chosen for them - Christianity. It might be worth noting that the third component which they recommend 'provides for individual development in course work for a project', but inequality has nonetheless already been built into the system by virtue of a prejudicial core and those who suffer are precisely those who are religiously undefended and possibly even at an educational disadvantage.

Both from the formal responses to questionnaires and from enlightened intuition, it would seem that the majority of classroom teachers of Religious Studies at CSE/GCE feel most comfortable with a predominantly Christian syllabus - not only for 16+ but, in fact, throughout the school. Why this is so is not entirely clear: it is doubtless due, in the case of Church schools, to the firm religious affiliation of the teachers, their pastoral responsibilities and their inability or unwillingness to differentiate between spiritual nurture and educational development. They are concerned with the 'wholeness' of the human personality and would see the distinction between the cognitive and the affective elements of religion and education as artificial and unacceptable. This is also true of some Religious Studies teachers in the maintained sector and not only those who have a tradition of Christian worship or who serve a worshipping community. Between them, they constitute a powerful pro-Christian lobby; but what is not certain is whether this lobby is merely acting to protect its own position and maintain a totally Christian-based syllabus, or whether it is crusading against others exercising the prerogative of following a syllabus which does not involve a study of Christianity at all. It would be quite inappropriate for Religious Studies, an optional subject within a system of public examinations in a multifaith society, to be manipulated in a missionary manner.

There is a strong and growing feeling among Religious Studies bodies - e.g., boards' advisory panels, subject associations, representatives of minority religious groups and the like - that an enforced study of Christianity is intolerable within a free and open society. The argument that Christianity is central to British culture is conceivably an argument for a study of Christianity within Religious Education as a school subject but that should not be confused with an optional subject at 16+: if the awareness of the Christian tradition were so vital for every child as to warrant compulsion, then it would seem most logical and most effective to include the course within a compulsory area of the school curriculum. If we are to take an objective view of Religious Studies, then we must accept that Christianity should occupy a central seat at 16+ only if the case could be made that religion could not be studied without it; or, possibly, that Christianity is the best exemplar of religion. This is clearly not plausible. Whatever individual Christians may believe and however strongly they personally hold to the supremacy (in spiritual or cultural terms) of Christianity as a faith, they cannot establish it as a supreme syllabus for study within the norms of Religious Studies. Needless to say, the same limitations would be placed on any life-stance that advanced its cause and tried to appropriate for itself special privileges and a favoured role.

There are several possible holds to break the deadlock. One is to abandon altogether the search for a common core of content, and to offer candidates an open, unrestricted selection from a series of discrete options which offered certain combinations (e.g., Old Testament and New Testament, Hinduism and Buddhism could either be offered separately or together). This is the approach now adopted and commended by the Joint Council's 16+ National Criteria Working Party for Religious Studies in their final report of January 1983. As their response to replies to their questionnaire and as a result of discussions and consultations, they have decided to reconsider the cultural case for compulsory Christianity and to separate those issues relating to the total curriculum from those which belong only to the examination syllabus. To be specific, the latest proposal is <u>either</u> a thematic study of three major world religions <u>or</u> a two-component option system (devoid of compulsion) involving <u>two</u> aspects of <u>one</u> major world religion or <u>one</u> aspect each of <u>two</u> major world religions. There are two disadvantages of this system: first, there is a possibility and a likelihood that most will opt for 'total' Christianity thereby dismissing the multicultural or multifaith perspective. Second, without a string to hold the beads together, there is a danger that the subject will not cohere. A common core of skills would prevent this.

Another solution is a common core framework which is representative of several traditions and equally fair to all individuals and which does so by drawing evenly from a number of life-stances. It could be likened to AEB's Multifaith syllabus, or London's Aspects of Five World Faiths or EA's Religion - a Thematic Approach. Such syllabuses would need to be reduced in scale to be taken in conjunction with an optional paper and to avoid becoming too superficial. This could be accomplished through a single, fairly self-contained religious dimension being explored through several traditions: Celebration of the Life-cycle or Annual Festivals would lend themselves to this broad treatment as there is an obvious element of common ground without the need for facile comparisons.

A corollary to this is the investigation of Religion as illustrated by religions. An example of this is given in Appendix B The Nature of Religion. Here the aims are those of the Joint Council's Religious Studies Working Party's Draft National Criteria and the specific objectives flow from them. The head of a Religious Studies department has produced the draft outline of content as a discussion document for a 16+ syllabus. The approaches adopted are variously anthropological, philosophical, psychological or sociological and this means that the syllabus is not without very serious conceptual difficulties and is too sophisticated in places. However, the value of such an approach is that it provides an opportunity to explore religious issues from a multicultural point of view. Specified content is kept to a bare minimum and this would offer teachers and pupils more control than usual over the selection of immediate material. The drawback of any thematic core, however, is that they contain material with which many teachers are unfamiliar and which they might either teach badly or not at all. Ultimately, it does not matter how effective a syllabus ought to be in promoting a warm acceptance of multiculturalism or an objective study of religion: if it does not win the support of teachers, for whatever reason, it is of no avail. Attitudes are always resistant to change even when there is an intellectual reason for doing so.

Another possibility is a modified form of the first: free options but with a difference. It is necessary to be realistic and to acknowledge the limits beyond which our multicultural aims cannot go: under such circumstances, free options - an à la carte menu of world religions, ethics, and scriptural texts - offer the line of least resistance and give less offence than any other system. The difference is in the way that the choices are patterned, and it might be helpful to think of a solution in terms of 'bags' and 'stones'; a 'bag' would represent a particular religious tradition and a 'stone' a dimension of it, for example:

Christianity	- to include New Testament; the Church today; etc.
Islam	- to include the Prophet Mohammad; Quranic law; etc.
Hinduism	- to include the Bhahagavad Gita; Hindu 'missionary' movements in the West; etc.

The proposal might be that candidates prepare for examination in an agreed number of 'stones' taken at will from the 'bags'. If the syllabus content is carefully structured now - in the present climate - it can be adapted (should the climate alter) with few complications by writing in a rubric that 'stones' must be picked from more than one 'bag'. The value of this is its relative painlessness as an operation in syllabus review and its provision of a stable 'interim ethic' which ensures continuity as well as an ultimate multicultural perspective. The difficulty lies in actually bringing about the change of climate, as a great deal has to do with inservice training; and here the examining boards could contribute to change.

Summary and conclusions

The central controversy concerns core Christianity: some advocate a Christian core with a compulsory element in another world religion (plus an individual option). Others suggest a Christian core with another option which *may* be more Christianity. The former proposal gives balance and a certain breadth but puts pupils from religious minorities at a disadvantage; the latter is prejudicial as well as weighted. Thematic cores will inevitably contain material which teachers are unable or unwilling to tackle. Free options are an apparently liberal solution but the subject loses coherence, and the problems of standardization are increased. This solution may also fail to challenge the deeply-entrenched focus upon Christianity in teaching which, on a large scale and over a long period of time, runs counter to multiculturalism.

Where reconciliation is impossible, compulsion is undesirable, and compromise unconscionable. An approach, therefore, is to devise a framework which is flexible enough to meet the desire for totally Christian syllabuses and the need for multicultural consciousness. The human element demands gradual weaning rather than force-feeding and so 'bags and stones' is offered here as a mixed diet capable of satisfying hunger while at the same time whetting the appetite for something more nourishing.

The question posed at the beginning of this chapter asked whether Religious Studies syllabuses should 'not only preserve the study of Christianity but also make it compulsory for candidates to study one other major religion'; 'not only' is a telling phrase: it implies that Christianity's special position *is* to be preserved and merely asks whether other experiences, traditions and elements have a place. The question begs the question.

V DISCUSSION POINTS FOR FUTURE DEVELOPMENTS

By way of concluding the arguments already made and the evidence presented, the author strongly commends the following thirteen specific courses of action for consideration. They are presented to the boards and others involved in 16+ development in the belief that if implemented they would contribute significantly to fulfilling the aims of multicultural assessment within Religious Studies.

1 Ends and means: a common core of skills

> The search for common content should be supplanted by a common core of skills.

One of the objections to the free-choice system is its lack of coherence. The more varied the content and the greater the number of possible combinations of options, the more crucial is the need for firm, clear aims and objectives in order to ensure consistency throughout the examination. The case for common skills is very strong: whatever the material involved in any given paper (or part of it) the same set of skills should be examined in dealing with it. Traditionally, the skills required of candidates have been very limited: undue emphasis has been laid on 'factual recall' and 'clarity of expression'. Other abilities must now come into play in order to test candidates' approaches to multiculturalism, such as, logical reasoning; understanding of symbol, ritual, and myth; detection of bias; adoption of objective standpoints.

2 Product and process: resource-based assessment

> Boards should supply stimulus material within examinations, whatever form they take.

It is vital to reduce the dependence on factual recall and to encourage critical awareness and reflective thought. These must be seen not as optional extras but as responses central to assessment within a multicultural society. It is not possible to test them entirely by means of a traditional written examination paper and therefore stimulus, resource-based questions can be put to imaginative use in eliciting reasoned reactions to the data offered.

3 Theory into practice: 'hands-on' assessment

> The feasibility of practical tests in Religious Studies should be seriously entertained by all boards, particularly in connection with living in a multifaith world.

If Religious Studies is truly about life, the teaching and learning of the subject will be oriented towards the existential and the experiential.

It therefore follows that examinations can only test what has been learned by adopting a similar approach. Discussion needs to be initiated into what counts as practical in the context of Religious Studies examinations; much of this will need to be school-based and may well draw upon pupil profiles, but the question remains as to whether, for example, a written observation of, say, an act of worship would suffice or whether participation is required. Conscientious objection would need to be accepted but the withdrawal of some candidates on that basis would present difficulties in standardization and award; however, these are difficulties which must be discussed and dealt with - not dodged.

The oral test is commended as a means of assessing social as well as intellectual skills (see Appendix C).

4 Accounting and accountability: monitoring Religious Studies examinations

> Boards should publish and make freely available data concerning the take-up of options.

One of the factors which has bedevilled this present study is the paucity of material relating to the popularity of optional papers. With one exception, boards either fail to collect such statistics or refuse to publish them. It would be most edifying to know, for instance, how many candidates are attracted to the 'progressive' papers and how many to the 'traditional'. It would also be useful to be given the separate success rates of the options: for example, many Religious Studies teachers enjoy preparing candidates for papers in 'personal relationships and social issues' (or an equivalent title) but many examiners will acknowledge unofficially that this is deceptively difficult, that many pupils are inadequately prepared for it and that the standard is very low.

5 Equal but different: parity among papers

> Great care should be taken to ensure that all optional papers are of the same style and difficulty.

This may seem too obvious a point to be stated but, at the moment, there are many examples of World Religions papers being much more complicated in format than traditional ones; such papers also tend to contain more sophisticated types of question, e.g., more essays and fewer questions requiring very limited responses. This practice is clearly introducing not only an uncontrolled variable but also an unfair cultural bias.

6 Universal and particular: reappraisal of denominational examinations

> The scope of concessional examinations should be extended to include all minority religions on offer within a given board, and these examinations should be known by the name of the religion and not as Religious Studies.

Despite ardent efforts to provide a broad-based Religious Studies at 16+ for all candidates, whatever their affiliation, there nevertheless remains a case for 'partisan papers'. It would be insensitive and unjust to abolish these papers as they have a powerful effect on the identity and commitment of the pupils who practise those religions. However, it might be professionally more accurate and culturally braver to devise a series of alternative subject titles (or sub-titles) for those narrow, specific choices of content, for example, Christian Studies, Islam, Judaica, Hindu Writings and so forth. Religious Studies would be reserved for a broader and bolder approach in which candidates demonstrate an ability and a willingness to approach more than one tradition.

7 Beginning in Bablyon: towards a Rastafarian syllabus

Steps should be taken to introduce a denominational syllabus in Rastafarianism.

This will not be easy but it must be worth the effort involved. There are two main difficulties: the first is that there are, at present, no examination syllabuses in Rastafarianism, very few books or other resources suitable for school use, and very few Religious Studies teachers who have developed curricula in Rastafarianism; the second is that the Rastafarian community may be reluctant to cooperate with examining boards and may well regard them as belonging to Babylon. Given that many Rastafarian youths will take some examinations at 16+, the possibility of an examination in their religion and culture may have an uplifting effect upon them and give them greater respectability and acceptance. Furthermore, the examination may well be taken by non-Rastafarian pupils, and this would increase its standing. It is to be hoped that a Rastafarian syllabus at 16+ will, in turn, generate curricular for the 11-14 age range and for non-examination groups aged 14-16. Furthermore, issues of prejudice and identity are marked here as they are in the case of Judaism and these make them very appropriate courses for non-Rastafarian and non-Jewish students respectively.

8 Reason and revelation: Christianity as a world religion

Christian syllabuses and examination papers should be treated impartially and externally.

It is inevitable - without being mandatory - that Christianity will form the greater part of most candidates' preparation for Religious Studies at 16+. Many Christian teachers and pupils will be tempted to treat the syllabus as an inner revelation and will not be prompted to see it with an enquiring mind and a critical eye. It may not be easy for them to abandon the idea of the primacy or supremacy of the Christian faith but they will be aided, in terms of preparation for an examination, if the boards do everything possible to present Christianity on the same level as other religions, to be viewed impartially. This is especially important in the case of Biblical options, where there is the risk that if the Christian Bible were offered as another option, the scope of the Christian material would be extended; this would distort the position of Christianity in the world, devaluing the Scriptures by removing them from the living religion of which they form a part, and putting non-Christian candidates at a disadvantage.

9 The one and the many: diversity within Christianity

Syllabuses and examinations should treat Christianity with due regard to its diversity.

Christianity is not monolithic, and examining boards, in accepting this, would not only do Christianity a great service but would also provide candidates with wider learning experiences, and themselves with more extensive examinable material.

There is within Christianity a considerable range of beliefs on doctrinal and ethical questions, despite various historic attempts at standardization and conformity, yet it is a universal religion in the sense that its adherents can be found in every country, and they represent the full gamut of human culture.

Syllabuses should not limit Christianity to its 'White' or 'British' phenomena but should expose the Christian experience in all its fullness, and - especially in the spirit of positive discrimination - accord a place of honour to the manifestations of Black Christian culture. The Black element should be encouraged, preferably stipulated, but, at the very least, allowed.

10 Others and otherness: material drawn from a variety of traditions

> The options on Prejudice and Community Relations should draw material from a number of religious traditions in syllabuses and examination papers and should be selected for their creative, constructive value.

It would be supremely ironic if the one area of Religious Studies which ostensibly holds the greatest potential for multicultural consciousness were, in reality, limited to a monocultural perspective. Virtually all boards at present - and there seems to be no move to change this - have a Religious Studies option which involves certain aspects of situation ethics - moral issues and concerns pertaining to contemporary society and the relationships between individuals. Whatever such sections may be called - that is, whether the word 'Christian' is used in the title or simply 'religions' - it is clear that the data-bank has very definitely been monofaith in the past: Christian examples from the teaching of Jesus, and excerpts from Church statements abound. This applies throughout the Social Issues section whether the topic is sexuality, international law, industrial management or, indeed, questions of ethnicity, racism, community relations or interfaith dialogue.

This need not be so, as there is a wealth of illustrative material on such matters within every tradition, and not to use it is a waste of human resources as well as a violation of multicultural aims.

11 Conscience and consciousness: the raising of issues

> All Religious Studies examinations should be flavoured with the richness and diversity of religious experience, and open to the values possessed, and issues posed, by religious evidence.

There will be some who, because of conflicts of conscience or limits of consciousness, will not yet be willing or able to entertain world faiths or the social implications of religious approaches to contemporary life. This is no reason to abandon - either in teaching or examining - the consideration of pluralism, for even within a single tradition these are multiple viewpoints and distinctive practices. Certainly, Biblical material is teeming with ideas and ideologies and lends itself to multicultural religious education and assessment.

12 'Bags' and 'stones': towards assessment in two traditions

> The 16+ Religious Studies syllabuses and examinations should be structured to offer free options now, with the eventual possibility of a rubric which would guarantee a two-tradition Religious Studies examination.

As explained at the end of Chapter IV, the ideal pattern for Religious Studies at 16+ involves two studies, at least one of which, by definition, cannot be the candidate's own tradition. It is equally clear that much re-education of knowledge and attitudes is called for and that, for the moment, an interim ethic must operate: sections for study could be loosely grouped together under one religion or theme. At a later date, it can be insisted that candidates do not choose both options from one religion. This is to enforce a modicum of breadth - enough to make the awareness of pluralism necessary - and to ensure that Religious Studies is not merely a reinforcement of sectarianism.

13 Vox pop: consultation with the community

> The various religious communities, especially minorities, should be consulted by the examining boards at every level and the boards' decisions should be taken in conjunction with the expressed needs and hopes of the communities.

This transcends mere tokenism and is the most important of all the considerations - the one which *must* be implemented if any headway is to be made; it celebrates the twin principles of mutual discovery and self-determination. It will not be until representatives of all faiths are present on Religious Studies advisory panels - until a Sikh is examiner in Sikhism or a Jew moderates a paper in Judaism - that we can begin to congratulate ourselves on assessment appropriate to a multicultural society. Without such invitations, we can never be sure that we are without bias or that we have not been guilty of stereotyping. At the moment, concessions to minorities are a 'gift' which we can offer or withhold at will and for which the minorities must be grateful. This is a system of patronage, not a democratic one, and it is quite insensitive to minority situations and aspirations. It is imperative that all people are enabled to define and determine themselves, and to this end examining boards must court their good will so that examiners, teachers, and students may begin to see others as they are and not as they suppose them to be.

The changes in Religious Studies which have already taken place and the further developments in Religious Studies assessment which are recommended in this pamphlet - be they evolutionary or revolutionary - have enormous implications for the initial and in-service training of teachers. At present, there are few religious minority teachers engaged in Religious Studies within state schools: the majority are Christian or 'post-Christian', and the responsibility of making multi-faith Religious Studies a classroom reality falls fairly on their shoulders. No help from colleges, university departments, Religious Education centres and examining boards can ever be too great.

We have come a long way. We have further to go.

REFERENCES

Attfield, D.G. (1974), 'The Justification of Assembly', *Learning for Living*, May, Christian Education Movement, 172-77

British Humanist Association (1975), *Objective, Fair and Balanced: A New Law for Religion in Education*, BHA

City of Birmingham Education Committee (1975), *Living Together*, City of Birmingham District Council

Cole, W.O. (1972), 'Religion in the Multi-Faith School', *Learning for Living*, November, Christian Education Movement, 23-26

Cole, W.O. (ed.) (1978a), *World Faiths in Education*, Allen and Unwin

Cole, W.O. (1978b), 'Towards a Total View of Religion in School', in Cole (1978a), 15-22

Cole, W.O. (1978c), 'Approaching Someone Else's Beliefs - Some Criteria', in Cole (1978a), 23-25

Cole, W.O. (1978d), 'Why World Religions - and Which? A Beginning, a Middle and an End', in Cole (1978a), 45-56

Cox, E. (1966), *Changing Aims in Religious Education*, Routledge and Kegan Paul

Cox, E. (1975), 'Principles Behind Syllabus Making', *Learning for Living*, March, Christian Education Movement, 132-33

Cox, E. (1976), 'Does It Do As It Says?', *Learning for Living*, summer, Christian Education Movement, 125-26

Davies, *et al.* (1979), *The Changing World and R.E.*, Centre for World Development Education

Durham Commission on Religious Education ('Durham' 1970), *The Fourth R*, Society for Promoting Christian Knowledge

Greenwood, W.N. and Marratt, H.W. (1977), *New Objective Tests in Religious Studies*, Hodder and Stoughton

Gryn, H. (1978), 'Religious Education in a Multicultural Society', *Trends in Education*, autumn, HMSO, 13-16

Hampshire Education Authority (1980), *Paths to Understanding*, Globe Education, Basingstoke

Hogbin, J. (1981), 'Towards National Criteria for a 16+ Examination in Religious Studies', in Lealman (1981), 13-28

Hull, J. (1974), Editorial, *Learning for Living*, May, Christian Education Movement, 170-71

Hull, J. (1976), Editorial, *Learning for Living*, March, Christian Education Movement, 130-31.

Hulmes, E. (1979), *Commitment and Neutrality in Religious Education*, Geoffrey Chapman

Jackson, R. (ed.) (1982), *Approaching World Religions*, John Murray

Joint 16+ Council Religious Studies Working Party (1983), *Report on Draft National Criteria for Religious Studies*, GCE and CSE Boards' Joint Council for 16+ National Criteria

Kelly, A.V. (editor) (1980a), *Curriculum Context*, Harper and Row

Kelly, A.V. (1980b), 'Ideological Constraints on Curriculum Planning' in Kelly (1980a)

Kidd J.B. (1982), Report on a National Conference: Examinations and Religious Education, held December 1981 at West Sussex Institute of Higher Education, Chichester (an occasional paper)

Lealman, B. (editor) (1981), *Current Issues in Examinations*, Christian Education Movement

Mansell, J. (1981), 'Student Profiles' in Lealman (1981),30-43

Marratt, H. (1981), '16+ Examination Proposals' in Lealman (1981), 8-11

Martin, D. (1977), 'Religious Education in a Secular Culture', *Learning for Living*, winter, Christian Education Movement, 58-65

Mills, I. (1976), 'Evaluating Different Religious Traditions' *Learning for Living*, autumn, Christian Education Movement,28-33

Newbigin, L. (1977), 'Teaching Religion in a Secular Plural Society', *Learning for Living*, winter, Christian Education Movement,82-88

Oliver, G. (1974), 'Religious Commitment and the Religious Education Teacher, *Learning for Living*, May, Christian Education Movement,181-83

Richardson, R. (1977), 'I Do Not Want To Be Here', *The New Era*, vol.61, no. 2, March/April 1980, 50-58

Richardson, R. (1982), 'World Studies and World Religions' in Jackson (1982), 182-91

Rivlin, H. (1973), Preface, Stent, Hazard and Rivlin (1973)

Schools Council (1971), *Religious Education in Secondary Schools* (Working Paper 36), Evans/Methuen Educational for Schools Council

Schools Council (1977), *Journeys into Religion*, Hart-Davis Educational for Schools Council

Schools Council (1981), *Towards National Criteria for a 16+ Examination in Religious Studies*, Report of the Religious Education Sub-committee

Schools Council (1981), *Education for a Multiracial Society: curriculum and context 5-15*, Schools Council Publications

Schools Council (1982), *Examining in a Multicultural Society*, report of conference held in 1981

Schools Council (1982), *Education of Children from Ethnic Minority Groups*, Pamphlet 19

Smart, N. (1968), *Secular Education and the Logic of Religion*, Faber

Smart, N. (1972), 'Comparative Religion Clichés', *Learning for Living*, November, Christian Education Movement, 4-7

Standing Advisory Council on Religious Education (1980), *Religious Education in Primary Schools in a Multicultural Society*, ILEA

Stent, N. Hazard, W.R. and Rivlin, H.N. (editors) (1973), *Cultural Pluralism in Education: A Mandate for Change*, Prentice Hall, New York

Stopes-Roe, H.V. (1976), 'The Concept of a "Life Stance" in Education', *Learning for Living*, autumn, Christian Education Movement, 25-28

Taylor, J. (1976), 'Initiation into Agnosticism', *Learning for Living*, summer, Christian Education Movement 129-30

Tibble, J.W. (1966), General Editor's Introduction in Cox (1966)

Wood, A. (1979), 'Judaism in the Home, Synagogue and Classroom', *Shap Mailing*, 7 Alderbrook Road, Solihull, West Midlands, 28-30

Woodward, P. (1973), 'Teaching World Religions', *Learning for Living*, March, Christian Education Movement, 21-24

Appendix A

THE GCE AND CSE EXAMINING BOARDS

The GCE Boards

Associated Examining Board (AEB)

Secretary: J. Day
Wellington House
Station Road
Aldershot
Hampshire GU11 1BQ

tel: 0252 25551

University of Cambridge Local Examinations Syndicate (Cambridge)

General Secretary: Dr F. Wild
Syndicate Buildings
17 Harvey Road
Cambridge CB1 2BU

tel: 0223 61111

Joint Matriculation Board (JMB)

Secretary: C. Vickerman
Manchester M15 6EU

tel: 061 273 2565

University of London School Examinations Department (London)

Secretary: A.R. Stephenson
66-72 Gower Street
London WC1E 6EE

tel: 01 636 8000

Oxford Delegacy of Local Examinations (Oxford)

Secretary: Miss C.G. Hunter
Oxford Delegacy of Local Examinations
Ewert Place
Summertown
Oxford OX2 7BZ

tel: 0865 54291

Oxford and Cambridge Schools Examination Board (O and C)

Secretary: A.R. Davis
Elsfield Way
Oxford OX2 8EP

tel: 0865 54421

Oxford and Cambridge Schools Examination Board (O and C)

Secretary: H.F. King
Brook House
10 Trumpington Street
Cambridge CB2 1QB

tel: 0223 64326

Southern Universities' Joint Board for School Examinations (SUJB)

Secretary: J. Symonds
Cotham Road
Bristol BS6 6DD

tel: 0272 36042

Welsh Joint Education Committee (WJEC)*

Secretary: J.L. Brace
Head of Examinations
Department: M. Jones
245 Western Avenue
Cardiff CF5 2YX

tel: 0222 561231

---

* CSE Board also.

The CSE Boards

Associated Lancashire Schools Examining Board (ALSEB)

Secretary: K. Tattersall
12 Harter Street
Manchester M60 7LH

tel: 061 228 0084/7

East Anglian Examinations Board (EA)

Secretary: Miss M.L. Thompson
The Lindens
Lexden Road
Colchester
Essex CO3 3RL

tel: 0206 49595

East Midland Regional Examinations Board (EM)

Secretary: D.J. Ramsden
Robins Wood House
Robins Wood Road
Aspley
Nottingham NG8 3NH

tel: 0602 295367

London Regional Examining Board (LR)

Secretary: D.H. Board
Lyon House
104 Wandsworth High Street
London SW18 4LF

tel: 01 870 3961

North Regional Examinations Board (NR)

Secretary: J.A. Winterbottom
Wheatfield Road
Westerhope
Newcastle upon Tyne NE5 5JZ

tel: 0632 862711

North-West Regional Examination Board (NW)

Secretary: J.E. Tipping
Orbit House
Albert Street
Eccles
Manchester M30 OWL

tel: 061 788 9521

South-East Regional Examinations Board (SE)

Secretary: P.N. Anderson
Beloe House
2-4 Mount Ephraim Road
Tunbridge Wells
Kent

tel: 0892 35311

Southern Regional Examinations Board (SR)

Secretary: H.G. Macintosh
Avondale House
33 Carlton Crescent
Southampton SO9 4YL

tel: 0703 32312

South-Western Examinations Board (SW)

Secretary: J. Edmundson
23-29 Marsh Street
Bristol BS1 4BP

tel: 0272 23434

West Midlands Examinations Board (WM)

Secretary: Dr G. Flack
Norfolk House
Smallbrook Queensway
Birmingham B5 4NJ

tel: 021 643 2081

West Yorkshire and Lindsey Regional Examining Board (WYL)*

Scarsdale House
136 Derbyshire Lane
Sheffield S8 8SE

tel: 0742 57436

Yorkshire Regional Examinations Board (YR)*

Secretary: B. Park
31-33 Springfield Avenue
Harrogate
Yorks HG1 2HW

tel: 0423 66991

---

* now merged to form the Yorkshire and Humberside Regional Examination Board

The Scottish Examination Board (Scotland)

The Director of the Board: J.H. Walker

Ironmills Road
Dalkeith
Midlothian EH22 1LE

tel: 031 663 6601

Northern Ireland Schools Examinations Council (NI)

GCE Board Secretary: S.W.W. Mercer
CSE Board Secretary: T. Jamison

Beechill House
42 Beechill Road
Belfast BT8 4RS

tel: 0232 647261

Appendix B

DRAFT 16+ SYLLABUS ON THE NATURE OF RELIGION

(prepared by the head of a Religious Studies department)

Objectives

1 To study religion as a component of human personality and as a contribution to human culture.

2 To ascertain and appreciate the diverse forms of religious exploration, explanation and expression.

Content

1 Religion and life's questions

Myths as a system of exploring and explaining the meaning of life: candidates to choose one (or two) questions to study through the medium of several myths.

2 Religion as a systematization of beliefs about God

A. The existence of God
   (i) reasons for acceptance
   (ii) reasons for rejection

B. Concepts of God
   (i) male and female
   (ii) God and nature
   (iii) God and human history

C. The one and the many: polytheism, monotheism, monism

D. Issues related to the.worship of God: holiness, anthropomorphism, idolatry

3 Religion in response to time

Ideas and experiences which stem from recorded moments:

A. The human life-cycle: birth, initiation, marriage, death

B. Weekly days of rest or worship

C. Cycle of seasons: spring, summer, autumn, winter

D. Historical events of joy or sorrow

4 Religion in response to space

Ideas and experiences which stem from recorded places

A. Awe-inspiring 'natural' places

B. Religious edifices and 'man-made' places which have assumed an awe-inspiring character

5 Religious experience and the individual

A. Ideas about body and soul

B. The sense of the numinous

C. Religion in solitude: the contemplative life

D. Visions of certain 'lone' prophets

6 Communal expressions of religion

A. Places of worship, homes and community houses

B. Mediators and ministers

C. Liturgy and ritual

D. Symbolic objects

E. Social action

7 Religion and morality

A. Morality 'with' and 'without' religion

B. Commandments and codes of conduct

C. Situation ethics

D. The idea of conscience

E. Moral teachings drawn from religious writings on certain themes: candidates should choose one or two themes to study through several traditions

8 What is religion?

Some definitions of religion, e.g., James, Marx, Freud

9 Religion and religions

A. Certain philosophical/epistemological considerations, e.g., is it still possible to know the truth? Are there 'true' or 'false' religions?

B. Interfaith dialogue

(i) organizations which aim at closer understanding between religious groups, e.g., World Congress of Faiths, World Council of Churches

(ii) issues of commitment, neutrality, tolerance, fanaticism

Appendix C

DRAFT MODE III CSE SYLLABUS ON ISLAM, AGREED BY A BOARD WITH SOME AMENDMENTS

Aims

The syllabus is intended to help pupils to:

1 study material which forms the basis of knowledge about Islam;

2 consider differing interpretations of that material with some sensitive awareness of its significance;

3 express clearly, relevantly, and honestly their own understanding of that material;

4 appreciate the nature of Islam and its contribution to communities and their values, especially with regard to:

(a) its chronological development
(b) its geographical spread
(c) its political power and force
(d) its permeation of the lives of Muslim individuals and families;

5 cultivate insight and reflection;

6 develop a respect for the beliefs and practices of Muslims.

Objectives

The examination is intended to test the ability of pupils to:

1 demonstrate knowledge of the key concepts and most important practices in Islam;

2 identify the principal Muslim beliefs and to explain the meanings given to them by Muslims;

3 perceive the relationship between belief and practice;

4 recognize various means of communication used within Islam;

5 identify and frame questions of ultimate value and social or personal concern;

6 express personal opinion, supported by evidence and argument, on issues raised by the study of Islam.

Syllabus content

1 Historical context

A. Arabia at the time of Mohammad

B. Life of Mohammad, with special reference to his revelations; the Hegira/Hijra; the establishment of the Muslim community in Yathrib/Medina, the conversion of the Meccans

C. Spread of Islam under the four caliphs

D. Shia and Sunni distinctiveness

E. Sufi developments

F. Establishments of madrasahs; rise of Islamic civilization in Egypt

G. Islam in the 20th century
  (1) 'Conversion' of Africa
  (2) Islamic Revival
  (3) Pan-Arabism and the 'problem of Israel'.

2 People and places

A. Prophets and the Muslim attitude towards them
  (1) Adam
  (2) Abraham
  (3) Ishmael
  (4) Moses
  (5) Jesus
  (6) Mohammad

B. Khadija and Fatima

C. Abu Bakr; Umar; Uthman; Ali

D. Khomeini; Arafat; Sadat

E. Mecca; Medina; Jerusalem

3 Sacred tradition

A. Qu'ran
B. Hadith
C. Sunna
D. Shari'a

4 Worship and festivals

A. Wudhu/wuzu: how and why

B. The mosque
  (1) the form of purpose-built mosques
  (2) requirements for the adaptation of buildings as mosques
  (3) the functions of mosques in Muslim life

C. Juma

D. Annual festivals
   (1) Eid-ul-Fitr
   (2) Eid-ul-Adha
   (3) Eid-Milad-ul-Nabi

5 Beliefs and practices

A. Recurring themes in Muslim life and thought
   (1) Oneness of God
   (2) Resistance to all forms of idolatry
   (3) Muslim community: unity and equality
   (4) Wholeness of Islam: a religion; a system of law; a way of life

B. Five Pillars of Islam
   (1) Shahadah
   (2) Salat
   (3) Siyyam
   (4) Zakat
   (5) Hajj

C. Jihad

D. Beliefs about the afterlife

6 Application in personal and social life

A. Islamic art and architecture: requirements governing style

B. Rites of passage
   (1) Birth and naming
   (2) Circumcision
   (3) Marriage
   (4) Death

C. Diet and dress

D. Attitudes to usury, gambling, and sexual behaviour

E. Islamic law concerning
   (1) Divorce
   (2) Women's rights
   (3) Political leadership
   (4) Crime and punishment

Scheme of Examination

Part	Marks	Weighting
Written Paper I	100	25%
Written Paper II	75	25%
Oral presentation and discussion	20	20%
Coursework	60	30%

Notes on examination scheme

Written paper I:

It is proposed that this paper will *not* allow for candidates' freedom of choice. There should be 25 short questions, each carrying 4 marks. These questions will test factual recall and some superficial application of ideas but will basically be of the objective variety. Space will be left on the question paper for candidates to write their answers. The suggested length of time for this paper is 1 hour.

Written paper II:

This paper will allow for some measure of candidates' choice and control. They will be required to attempt 3 questions from a total of 6 set on discrete topics. Each topic question will be of several scaled parts (i.e., of progressive difficulty) and the marks available for each part of a question will be clearly shown on the examination paper. However, candidates will be expected to attempt *all* the parts of the questions they have chosen. A total of 25 marks will be available for each question. Answers will be written on blank paper. 1½ hours should be allotted to this paper.

Oral presentation and discussion:

This will follow the format of certain examinations in Social Studies and other subjects. Candidates will be required to prepare a presentation lasting not more than 5 minutes on a deeper/alternative study of a section of the syllabus. The presentation may be read/spoken to the whole teaching group and may employ visuals where appropriate. Considerable scope will be afforded candidates in this part of the examination and it is intended to be an independent piece of work. However, teacher guidance will be offered especially in the original choice of topic and in the selection of material. Following the presentation by an individual candidate, the topic will be discussed by the whole group and the presenter will be expected to answer questions, respond to comments and counter criticism. The class teacher will be present, as will another teacher - preferably a Religious Studies specialist but, if not, a Humanities teacher who is accustomed to this mode of teaching/examining - and together they will assess individual candidates on (a) their presentation of the topic chosen; (b) their handling of the discussion of their topic; and (c) their contribution to the discussion of other candidates' presentations. The presentations and discussions will be recorded on standard audio cassette tape and made available to the board.

Courework:

Candidates will select for inclusion in their assessment pieces of work already completed during the course and already marked by the teacher. The pieces of work will be either 'short' or 'long': e.g., limited notes on a given subject or comments on a film or visit will qualify as 'short'; whereas only a more extended essay or a simple piece of research requiring some initiative and insight could be counted as 'long'. Candidates will be awarded a total possible of 5 marks for each 'short' piece submitted and 10 for each 'long' piece - up to a total maximum of 60 marks (e.g., 12 'short'; or 6 'long'; or 3 'long' and 6 'short' etc.).

PROGRAMME 5 MONITORING AND REVIEW GROUP

A.H. Jennings (Chairman)	Formerly Headmaster, Ecclesfield School, Sheffield; acting Chairman, Schools Council (Secondary Heads Association)
R. Aitken	Director of Education, Coventry (Association of Metropolitan Authorities)
SI B.C. Arthur	HM Inspectorate of Schools
J.J. Billington	Deputy Headmaster, High Pavement Sixth Form College, Nottingham (Assistant Masters and Mistresses Association)
D. Foster (to December 1981)	Headmaster, Churchill School, Bristol (CSE examining boards)
W.S. Frearson (from March 1982)	Ashford College, Middlesex (CSE examining boards)
J.C. Hedger	Department of Education and Science
P.M. Herbert	The Elliott School, London SW15 (National Association of Schoolmasters/Union of Women Teachers)
H.F. King (from April 1982)	Secretary, Oxford and Cambridge Schools Examination Board (GCE examining boards)
D.I. Morgan	Vice-principal, W.R. Tuson College, Preston, Lancs (National Union of Teachers)
R. Potts	Harraby Comprehensive School, Carlisle (National Union of Teachers)
A.R. Stephenson (to March 1982)	Secretary, University of London School Examinations Department (GCE examining boards)

PROJECT STEERING GROUP AND PROFESSIONAL SUPPORT

Project steering group

F. Cummins (Chairman)	Headteacher, Thomas Telford High School, Sandwell	*representing CSE examining boards*
H. Kelly (from January 1983)	Secretary, Association of LEA Advisory Officers for Multicultural Education	*representing LEAs*
E. Parsons	Deputy Headteacher, Whitley Abbey School, Coventry	*representing teachers*
C. Power (to September 1982)	Multicultural Adviser, London Borough of Haringey	*representing LEAs*
A. Shaffer	Lecturer in Sociology, Kingsway Princeton College, London WC1	*representing GCE examining boards*
P. Singh	HM Inspectorate of Schools	

Schools Council

G. Bardell (Lead officer)	Assessment and Examinations Team	
A. Craft	Coordinator for Multicultural Education	
G. Insull (from August 1982)	Administrative support	
S. Phillips	Lecturer in German, Cross Keys Tertiary College, Gwent	*representing Modern Languages Committee*
P. Scott (to July 1982)	Administrative support	
B. Thompson	Science teacher, St Paul's RC School, Leicester	*representing Working Party on Multicultural Education*

Professional support

Community language consultants

M. Roussou	Greek Coordinator Schools Council Mother Tongue Project
R. Russell	Emeritus Reader in Urdu School of Oriental and African Studies, University of London

External readers

B. Allison	Professor of Art Education, Leicester Polytechnic	*Art and design*
R. Bruce	Secondary Adviser in Religious Education, Inner London Education Authority	*Religious studies*
P. Burdett	Copthall Girls' School, London NW7	*Biology*
M. Christodoulides	Assistant Examiner, School Examinations Department, University of London	*Community languages: modern Greek*
E. Gray	Head of English, Wakefield Girls' High School	*English*
Dr R. McGregor	Lecturer in Hindi, Faculty of Oriental Studies, University of Cambridge	*Community languages: Hindi*
R. Russell	Emeritus Reader in Urdu School of Oriental and African Studies, University of London	*Community languages: Urdu*
I. Shelton	Deputy Headteacher, Sale Girls' Grammar School, Trafford	*Social sciences*
Dr B. Tolley	Lecturer in Education, University of Nottingham	*History*
M. Walshe	Staff Inspector, Inner London Education Authority	*Home economics*